A Retreat With Thea Bowman and Bede Abram

# Other titles in the
# A Retreat With... *Series:*

# A Retreat With
# Thea Bowman and Bede Abram

## *Leaning On the Lord*

Joseph A. Brown, S.J.

**ST. ANTHONY MESSENGER PRESS**
Cincinnati, Ohio

Scripture citations are taken from *New Revised Standard Version Bible*, copyright ©1989 by the Division of Christian Education of the National Council of Churches of Christ in the U.S.A. and used by permission.

Excerpt from *John of the Cross: Selected Writings*, ed. Kieran Kavanaugh, O.C.D., copyright ©1987 by Paulist Press, is reprinted by permission of Paulist Press.

Excerpt from *The Collected Works of St. Teresa of Avila*, trans. Kieran Kavanaugh and Otilio Rodriguez, copyright ©1976 by the Washington Province of Discalced Carmelites, ICS Publications, 2131 Lincoln Road, N.E., Washington, D.C. 20002. Reprinted by permission.

Excerpts from Thea Bowman's introduction to *Lead Me, Guide Me: The African-American Catholic Hymnal*, copyright ©1987 by G.I.A. Publications, are reprinted by permission of the publisher.

Excerpts from "Lord, Let Me Live Til I Die" by Fabvienen Taylor (*Praying*, November-December, 1989) are reprinted by permission of *Praying*.

The excerpt from *The Spirituals and the Blues* by James H. Cone (Orbis Books, 1991), copyright ©1972, 1991 by James H. Cone, is reprinted by permission of Orbis Books.

The excerpt from Catholic News Service (May 19, 1988) is reprinted by permission of Catholic News Service.

The excerpt from "Sister Lou" in *The Collected Poems of Sterling A. Brown*, copyright ©1980 by Sterling A. Brown, is reprinted by permission of HarperCollins Publishers.

The excerpt from "The Sanctified Church" in *Zora Neale Hurston: Folklore, Memoirs, and Other Writings*, copyright ©1983 by Everette Hurston, Sr., is reprinted by permission of HarperCollins Publishers.

Cover illustration by Steve Erspamer, S.M.
Cover and book design by Mary Alfieri
Electronic format and pagination by Sandra Digman

ISBN 0-86716-277-5

Published by St. Anthony Messenger Press
Printed in the U.S.A.

# Contents

# *Introducing* A Retreat With...

Twenty years ago I made a weekend retreat at a Franciscan house on the coast of New Hampshire. The retreat director's opening talk was as lively as a long-range weather forecast. He told us how completely God loves each one of us—without benefit of lively anecdotes or fresh insights.

As the friar rambled on, my inner critic kept up a sotto voce commentary: "I've heard all this before." "Wish he'd say something new that I could chew on." "That poor man really doesn't have much to say." Ever hungry for manna yet untasted, I devalued any experience of hearing the same old thing.

After a good night's sleep, I awoke feeling as peaceful as a traveler who has at last arrived safely home. I walked across the room toward the closet. On the way I passed the sink with its small framed mirror on the wall above. Something caught my eye like an unexpected presence. I turned, saw the reflection in the mirror and said aloud, "No wonder he loves me!"

This involuntary affirmation stunned me. What or whom had I seen in the mirror? When I looked again, it was "just me," an ordinary person with a lower-than-average reservoir of self-esteem. But I knew that in the initial vision I had seen God-in-me breaking through like a sudden sunrise.

At that moment I knew what it meant to be made in the divine image. I understood right down to my size eleven feet what it meant to be loved exactly as I was. Only later did I connect this revelation with one granted to the Trappist monk-writer Thomas Merton. As he reports in *Conjectures of a Guilty Bystander*, while standing all unsuspecting on a street corner one day, he was overwhelmed by the "joy of being...a member of a race in which God Himself became incarnate.... There is no way of telling people that they are all walking around shining like the sun."

As an absentminded homemaker may leave a wedding ring on the kitchen windowsill, so I have often mislaid this precious conviction. But I have never forgotten that particular retreat. It persuaded me that the Spirit rushes in where it will. Not even a boring director or a judgmental retreatant can withstand the "violent wind" that "fills the entire house" where we dwell in expectation (see Acts 2:2).

So why deny ourselves any opportunity to come aside awhile and rest on holy ground? Why not withdraw from the daily web that keeps us muddled and wound? Wordsworth's complaint is ours as well: "The world is too much with us." There is no flu shot to protect us from infection by the skepticism of the media, the greed of commerce, the alienating influence of technology. We need retreats as the deer needs the running stream.

### An Invitation

This book and its companions in the *A Retreat With...* series from St. Anthony Messenger Press are designed to meet that need. They are an invitation to choose as director some of the most powerful, appealing and wise mentors our faith tradition has to offer.

Our directors come from many countries, historical

eras and schools of spirituality. At times they are teamed to sing in close harmony (for example, Francis de Sales, Jane de Chantal and Aelred of Rievaulx on spiritual friendship). Others are paired to kindle an illuminating fire from the friction of their differing views (such as Augustine of Hippo and Mary Magdalene on human sexuality). All have been chosen because, in their humanness and their holiness, they can help us grow in self-knowledge, discernment of God's will and maturity in the Spirit.

Inviting us into relationship with these saints and holy ones are inspired authors from today's world, women and men whose creative gifts open our windows to the Spirit's flow. As a motto for the authors of our series, we have borrowed the advice of Dom Frederick Dunne to the young Thomas Merton. Upon joining the Trappist monks, Merton wanted to sacrifice his writing activities lest they interfere with his contemplative vocation. Dom Frederick wisely advised, "Keep on writing books that make people love the spiritual life."

That is our motto. Our purpose is to foster (or strengthen) friendships between readers and retreat directors—friendships that feed the soul with wisdom, past and present. Like the scribe "trained for the kingdom of heaven," each author brings forth from his or her storeroom "what is new and what is old" (Matthew 13:52).

## *The Format*

The pattern for each *A Retreat With...* remains the same; readers of one will be in familiar territory when they move on to the next. Each book is organized as a seven-session retreat that readers may adapt to their own schedules or to the needs of a group.

Day One begins with an anecdotal introduction called "Getting to Know Our Directors." Readers are given a telling glimpse of the guides with whom they will be sharing the retreat experience. A second section, "Placing Our Directors in Context," will enable retreatants to see the guides in their own historical, geographical, cultural and spiritual settings.

Having made the human link between seeker and guide, the authors go on to "Introducing Our Retreat Theme." This section clarifies how the guides are especially suited to explore the theme and how the retreatant's spirituality can be nourished by it.

After an original "Opening Prayer" to breathe life into the day's reflection, the author, speaking with and through the mentor(s), will begin to spin out the theme. While focusing on the guides' own words and experience, the author may also draw on Scripture, tradition, literature, art, music, psychology or contemporary events to illuminate the path.

Each day's session is followed by reflection questions designed to challenge, affirm and guide the reader in integrating the theme into daily life. A "Closing Prayer" brings the session full circle and provides a spark of inspiration for the reader to harbor until the next session.

Days Two through Six begin with "Coming Together in the Spirit" and follow a format similar to Day One. Day Seven weaves the entire retreat together, encourages a continuation of the mentoring relationship and concludes with "Deepening Your Acquaintance," an envoi to live the theme by God's grace, the directors' guidance and the retreatant's discernment. A closing section of Resources serves as a larder from which readers may draw enriching books, videos, cassettes and films.

We hope readers will experience at least one of those memorable "No wonder God loves me!" moments. And we hope that they will have "talked back" to the mentors, as good friends are wont to do.

A case in point: There was once a famous preacher who always drew a capacity crowd to the cathedral. Whenever he spoke, an eccentric old woman sat in the front pew directly beneath the pulpit. She took every opportunity to mumble complaints and contradictions—just loud enough for the preacher to catch the drift that he was not as wonderful as he was reputed to be. Others seated down front glowered at the woman and tried to shush her. But she went right on needling the preacher to her heart's content.

When the old woman died, the congregation was astounded at the depth and sincerity of the preacher's grief. Asked why he was so bereft, he responded, "Now who will help me to grow?"

All of our mentors in *A Retreat With...* are worthy guides. Yet none would seek retreatants who simply said, "Where you lead, I will follow. You're the expert." In truth, our directors provide only half the retreat's content. Readers themselves will generate the other half.

As general editor for the retreat series, I pray that readers will, by their questions, comments, doubts and decision-making, fertilize the seeds our mentors have planted.

And may the Spirit of God rush in to give the growth.

*Gloria Hutchinson*
*Series Editor*
*Conversion of Saint Paul, 1995*

# Getting to Know Our Directors

Though it would not be considered an "old Negro Spiritual," the favorite Baptist hymn, "Sometimes a Light Surprises," could very easily sum up my introduction to both Sister Thea Bowman and Father Bede Abram. The hymn's first stanza says:

> Sometimes a light surprises
> The Christian while he sings;
> It is the Lord who rises
> With healing in his wings.
> When comforts are declining,
> He grants the soul again
> A season of clear shining,
> To cheer it after rain.[1]

At the end of a cold, drizzly day in Techny, Illinois, where the National Association of Black Catholic Administrators (NABCA) had invited me to speak at their 1985 national gathering, we went into the chapel for evening prayer. Earlier, at the reception, while I had been enthusiastically renewing old acquaintances with colleagues and friends, I noticed the arrival of a strange-looking woman who seemed to be navigating her progress along the fringe of the gathering. A tall, dark-skinned person, she was dressed for maximum warmth in the Chicago-area November cold. A long coat, a head-wrap, gloves and boots gave her the appearance of someone who took my grandmother's admonition seriously: "In the winter, if you have to choose between being pretty and being warm, choose warm." This tall stranger was carrying two shopping bags and had an intense gaze that seemed more disturbing than inviting.

I was soon called back from the peripheral notice that I had given to her, and my friends and I made our way to the chapel. Just as the crowd fell into that universal quieting down that occurs at the beginning of every church service I have ever attended, a loud and raw moaning began in the back of the chapel. I could not help but turn to see what was erupting at that solemn moment. The same tall, dark-skinned woman who had disconcerted me at the reception was sitting in the last row of the congregants, rocking from side to side and uttering a truly unsettling vocalise. I asked one of my friends, "Who is that woman? She's dressed like a bag lady off the streets, and she looks half crazy to me."

The response given me by Father J-Glenn Murray was a look of disbelief and shock.

"Do you mean you don't know who that is?"

"No. I've never seen her before in my life."

"That's Sister Thea Bowman," J-Glenn told me. He went on, whispering, "I thought everybody in the world knew Thea by now. People either love her or loathe her," he said. "I decided it was altogether easier to love her. So I do."

Sometimes a light surprises, indeed. I had been away from the works of the National Black Catholic leadership organizations while involved in my doctoral studies and teaching in a college in the Midwest. I had not known Thea, had never heard her soaring and overwhelming voice, had not known of the "sayings and doings" of Sister Thea. As the prayer service progressed and she led the assembly in wonderful evocations of another time, place and climate—as she brought Mississippi and Georgia and

Virginia and Louisiana into the winter time of our meeting—I did what any good friend would do: I trusted the judgment of someone I respected. I decided that a "Sister Thea" was a good experience, though an unsettling one.

Two years earlier I had been approached to consider teaching at the newly organized Black Theology program offered by Xavier University in New Orleans. Father Joseph Nearon, S.S.S., the director of the Institute for Black Catholic Studies in 1984, had asked me to visit the program to see if we could develop a mutual interest in my joining the faculty. Tragically, Father Nearon died before I could pursue his invitation, and I thought nothing more of it. What I did not know during my participation at the NABCA meeting in Techny in 1985 was that Thea Bowman had put me under a scrutiny every bit as rigorous as the one I had been employing upon her. She decided, based on my performance at the gathering, that I needed to be a part of the Institute enterprise, and she took it upon herself to make her intentions known and realized.

At Christmas, I received a charming note from Thea Bowman and proceeded to ignore it, as I do most of my correspondence (until some external motive forces me to do the right thing). In late January, very early in the morning, while I was still sleeping, my telephone rang and a voice full of genuine humor said, "This is Thea Bowman. Don't you ever answer your mail? Your mama told me that you like to sleep late and that I should call you real early in the morning if I wanted to get you. Well, were you asleep?"

"Sometimes a Light surprises... It is the Lord who rises with healing in his wings." Sister Thea went on to invite me to come to New Orleans for the next summer session of the Institute for Black Catholic Studies. She wanted me to team-teach a course with her, "The Spirituality of Black Literature." She assured me that I would find the experience grace-filled, that she was convinced that I belonged at the Institute and she told me that the new director of the Institute would contact me and make all the formal arrangements. And it came to pass just as she announced.

I arrived in New Orleans the night before classes began. That evening Thea and I sat on a bench outside the chapel and talked for just under a half-hour. The next morning I found our classroom and my life changed forever.

Since I was more or less a visitor, I decided to have a full immersion experience of the Institute for Black Catholic Studies, choosing to sit in all the classes being taught, so that I could meet a group of brilliant, talented women and men who had hitherto been mostly unknown to me. And that decision further rearranged the boundaries of my known universe. I was astonished at the level of teaching going on in each of the classrooms. Sister Delores Harrell walked into her "Catholic Education in the Black Community" class and overwhelmed us with the elegance of her mind and body. Dr. Nathan Jones performed his lectures in catechetics, teaching by example and lifting up his students to new heights of excellence. Father Cyprian Davis gave a steadying foundation to our restored Catholic history, and his dry wit and infectious enthusiasm delighted my senses.

And then there was Bede.

In *The Souls of Black Folk*, W.E.B. Du Bois evokes the memory of his first encounter with African American religion as practiced in the rural areas of Tennessee in the late nineteenth century. Du Bois, a fourth-generation Episcopalian from Massachusetts, was attending Fisk University when he went into the countryside to teach rural black folks as a part of his curriculum requirements. What Du Bois remembers of his first encounter with the religion of his students expresses the consternation and attraction I felt when Father Bede Abram burst into his classroom my first morning at the Institute. Du Bois says:

> And so most striking to me, as I approached the village and the little plain church perched aloft, was the air of intense excitement that possessed that mass of black folk. A sort of suppressed terror hung in the air and seemed to seize us,—a pythian madness, a demoniac possession, that lent terrible reality to song and word. The black and massive form of the preacher swayed and quivered as the words crowded to his lips and flew at us in singular eloquence.[2]

Bede Abram waited outside the classroom until it was exactly time to begin. And then he burst into the room, flinging his books onto his desk, shouting—no, *screaming*—"Somebody stole my shoes. Somebody stole my shoes." Like the old song says, "I went to the rock to hide my face, and the rock cried out, 'No hiding place!'" There was no place to run, no place to hide. Words tumbled, hurtled, collided like particles in an atom-smasher; and that was the intention of Bede, his method and his "madness." The song and the word of Black Theology is confrontational, sudden and irresistible. The messenger, the message and the medium converged, and took all of us in that room to a place dreamed of only in Revelation.

Bede Abram did not fit the "form" of Du Bois' preacher. Bede was slender—slight, actually—and nervous, almost manic, in his gestures and countenance. Words like "quicksilver" (and its cousin, "mercurial") must be redeemed from the status of cliché in order to capture a portion of his effect. Punctuating his every talk,

11

workshop or lecture were the ever-present cigarette and some sort of liquid caffeine-provider. Illustrating the law of physics concerning objects remaining in motion, Bede stalked the subject matter and the recipients of his brilliance. During that summer he engaged in his usual practice of teaching three classes a day, while I went for a nap after my first encounter with him.

But nothing could ever rest again inside my mind. That part of our cultural and theological inheritance which I had treasured and protected in an intellectual manner seemed lifeless and desiccated when I watched Bede sit in a chair and *become* the songs of our ancestors as they were transported in the festering holds of the slaving ships. The moans and howlings coming from his throat were identical to those haunting the classroom of Thea Bowman that summer. What had been liberating concepts on the pages of books in the libraries of my school in New Haven became vibrant spirit-possession ceremonies of healing and restoration in the semitropical settings of New Orleans.

My first summer meeting with Thea and Bede became "a season of clear shining." Sometimes a light surprises. I am able to read the account of Ezra reading the Law of Moses to the exiles returning to Jerusalem (Nehemiah 9— 10) and feel the same revival of the spirit that those exiles must have felt. Thea Bowman, F.S.P.A., and Bede Abram, O.F.M. Conv., were evangelists and prophets in the most biblical understanding of the word. Both were angels/ messengers filled with the awe-inspiring and awe-filled word of God, whose songs were like bright and shining swords, cleaving the air and pointing to heaven. They were supremely well-educated and well-trained in the pedagogical techniques of African American studies. They were also faithful to the Franciscan charisms in which their ministry and service were rooted. Peripatetic and earthy, simultaneously eloquent and rough in their pursuit of excellence, plainspoken and humble in the face of challenges, both Thea and Bede brought to all who heard them a challenge to see and hear with new ears and eyes an old and often neglected story of the most authentic "theology of liberation" known to our culture.

## *Placing Our Directors in Context*

Sister Thea Bowman, F.S.P.A., and Father Bede Abram, O.F.M. Conv., were exact contemporaries, devoted colleagues and, most in keeping with the tradition begun by Francis and Clare, bonded, soul to soul, as sister and brother. In classrooms, from stages, at the altar and at the pulpit, in celebrations of every kind Thea Bowman and Bede Abram were singing and dancing "canticles of praise." The love and affection they shared with each other spilled over, forming a community among those who gathered around them. Blended joy and sorrow, approbation and admonition were part of their witnessed conversation and concerns. In the most informal—and therefore deeply rooted—ways, each referred to the other as "sister," or "brother," recognizing that the vowed life to which each was committed created new circles of support, new constellations of *family*.

### Sister Thea

In 1937 Sister Thea entered into the world as Bertha J. Bowman, the daughter of Theon E. Bowman, a medical doctor serving the community of Canton, Mississippi, and his wife Mary E. Coleman Bowman, a schoolteacher. Thea was, as she often said, "an old folks' child," having been born to older parents and growing up in an environment filled with elders, all of whom—grandparents, neighbors, teachers—filled her life with the songs, stories and values of the culturally rich African American community of the rural South. When the education offered by the public school system failed this obviously gifted child, Thea's mother enrolled her in a Catholic school that had been recently staffed by the Franciscan Sisters of Perpetual Adoration, a community of women religious whose headquarters were in La Crosse, Wisconsin—in many ways, the polar opposite direction of Canton.

Bertha Bowman's intellect and religious sensibilities were quickened by the care and example of these hardworking and self-sacrificing women. At the age of ten, she informed her parents of her desire to become a Roman Catholic. Six years later, she left Canton, journeying to La Crosse to enter religious life and to continue her progress toward becoming the teacher, evangelist, scholar and caretaker of culture known and venerated around the world as Sister Thea.

Thea Bowman's teaching career was as thorough and as comprehensive as can be imagined. From 1958 until her death in 1990, she "gathered the little children" to her (and all who sat in her learning environments became children, no matter their chronological age). After years teaching at the elementary level, in both La Crosse and in Canton, Thea went to The Catholic University of America in Washington, D.C., to begin her graduate studies in English literature. Her enthusiasm for philosophy, rhetoric and aesthetics was honed to a fine finish during these years (1968-1972), and forever afterwards the words of Aristotle, Thomas Aquinas and Erasmus were quoted in her lectures and conversation along with the lyrics of bawdy Delta blues and the aphorisms of a ubiquitous and often apocryphal "old lady."

It was the lessons learned from the "old ladies" and

the "old gentlemen" of her childhood and youth that sustained and informed Sister Thea's spirituality and scholarship. We might imagine that, when she journeyed to the Franciscan novitiate in La Crosse, she carried with her a "spiritual quilt" of songs, stories, beliefs, wise words and attitudes with which she could keep herself warm, comforted and consoled. (In a 1987 interview, Thea recalled that when she joined the Catholic Church in the 1940's, "we had to leave behind us the music that was an expression of the spirituality of our home, community and upbringing." However, she added, that strict emphasis on liturgical uniformity was eradicated by Vatican II.[3])

The various experiences and memories of Sister Thea's diverse education became a work of great value as she brought forth from her "storeroom treasures old and new." In a process akin to the great unitive experiences of the mystics of the European Middle Ages, Thea Bowman became the "old lady" who was her authoritative reference in so many of her lectures and observations.

It was the *persona* of the old lady dispensing wisdom, love and guidance that transformed the last six years of her life. As she carried the seeds of physical death in her body, she continued to move about the world telling folks how to live until they died. As she told a reporter in the spring of 1988, she felt "God has planned something. I don't always understand it, but like the black spiritual says, his eye is on the sparrow and I know he's watching me."[4] She had been diagnosed with breast cancer in 1984. Several periods of remission followed. Then Thea's final battle with bone cancer forced her from a wheelchair to her bed. Incapacitated in body and sometimes unable to pray, Sister Thea relied on audiotapes of her favorite spirituals to "pray for her." She died on March 30, 1990.[5]

## Father Bede

In the death notice prepared for Father Bede Abram by his Conventual Franciscan community (the St. Anthony of Padua Province), it is said that "Father Bede was known for his enthusiasm for life, learning, preaching, and teaching. His gentle smile and booming voice were gifts he readily shared." The gifts behind the gifts were nurtured in a crucible of black experience in its rawest forms for much of his life and ministry. The complexity of the art form known as "the blues" can symbolize much of Bede Abram's life, ministry and meaning. Sometimes, as one of the blues songs says, "you've got to laugh to keep from crying." Bede's booming voice was used deliberately and masterfully to prophetic effect. His gentle smile was hard-earned and filled with grace. It was a sign that many of the demons who haunted the wilderness of his life had been held at bay by his fierce spirituality and loyalty to his family and to his African American heritage.

Born in Buffalo, New York, in 1942, and trained by his Franciscan community in Maryland, Massachusetts and New York, Bede was, ultimately, a child of the South. His inflections, his references, his style of preaching, teaching and counseling were shaped and refined by his extended family and the wide circle of his friends who were deeply rooted in Southern soil and culture. His intellect could only have been called precocious by all who knew him from a very early age. His mind absorbed information, nuances and details. He had a poet's ear and an actor's eye for observing how people spoke, moved and interacted, and he also had an artist's ability to reflect back to his listener the "telling effect" in order to evangelize more thoroughly.

His education, after he joined the Order of Friars Minor Conventual in 1961, was familiar to the Catholic world immediately preceding the changes wrought by Vatican Council II. By the time of his ordination in 1971, Bede Abram had immersed himself in the classic issues of philosophy and theology learned by clerics everywhere in America at that time. That he had excelled in his studies and added to his storehouse of knowledge all he could glean from the wealth of texts and theories exploding during the Black Renaissance of the late 1960's and early 1970's was immediately evident to all who heard him. He had a special gift for making even the most complex theological abstractions pithy and pertinent to widely divergent audiences.

Bede traveled the country for the nineteen years of his priesthood, teaching and preaching with something bordering on the "frenzy" described above by Du Bois. Until his health failed him shortly before his death, he devoted his considerable energy to confronting ignorance and fear in the pews of (still) mostly segregated Catholic churches. His commitment to the Institute for Black Catholic Studies, for which he was (along with Thea Bowman) a member of the founding faculty, was also unlimited. After suffering a series of heart attacks, Bede would leave his sickbed to get to his summer classes. Later he was so debilitated he could not leave his apartment, so he held his classes in his living room. Bede Abram gave and "never counted the cost"; he challenged his students to do the same when embracing the richness of Black Theology and Black culture.

Confrontation and challenge were the touchstones of Bede's style of teaching and preaching. Those qualities were leavened with humor, compassion and an identification with Christ the Suffering Servant that made him a profoundly loyal friend, confidant and advisor to hundreds of men and women. There are many white priests, nuns and lay educators whose first experience of

Black Theology was a lecture or a workshop given by Bede Abram and who would be able to say, with the disciples on the road to Emmaus, "Were not our hearts burning within us while he was talking to us on the road...?" (Luke 24:32). And these same Church leaders would attest to the essential change of perspective effected in them by his call to conversion and his demand that all who would see Christ look in the hearts and faces of the often-despised other.

The members of Bede's extended family, women and men who had suffered through rejection, abuse, betrayals, lynchings and immeasurable heart-grief, possessed him when he taught and preached. Their lives allowed him to see his worth and to claim his freedom as a child of God. His joy and his pain were equally precious to him, as they were to his beloved friend, Thea Bowman. Both Bede and Thea manifested a holy and consuming devotion to each other, to all who came to them for instruction and to the Catholic Church.

The day before Thea died, she spoke with Bede and helped him with his grieving. They were brother and sister to each other, giving witness even as they left this world that love endures. Bede was the presiding cleric at Thea's funeral in Jackson, Mississippi, focusing for the entire congregation how leave-taking should be done. Even on that day, the reality of the brief flame of life that is allotted to some was uppermost in Bede's mind. He remarked to several of his friends at that time that he would not survive Thea by many months. Less than a year later, on January 20, 1991, in New Orleans, Bede Abram died.

Both Thea Bowman and Bede Abram are present in many homes, classrooms and faith communities years after their deaths. Their writings, the tapes of their lectures and sermons, the anecdotes that punctuate the gatherings of thousands of their generation of friends, associates and listeners have served to root them in the faith development of a truly *catholic* Church. May what follows, distilled from an experience of their faith and spirit, enable others to "come out the wilderness, leaning on the Lord," strengthened with the songs and prayers, filled with the hope and energy that led and guided Thea and Bede.

## Notes

[1] *Baptist Hymnal* (Nashville, Tenn.: Convention Press, 1975), #221.

[2] W.E.B. Du Bois, *The Souls of Black Folk* (New York: Vintage Books/The Library of America, 1990), p. 211.

[3] *The New York Times*, April 1, 1990, p. 23.

[4] National Catholic News Service, May 19, 1988.

[5] A thorough chronology of the major events of Sister Thea's life appears in *Sister Thea Bowman, Shooting Star: Selected Writings and Speeches*, ed. Celestine Cepress (Winona, Minn.: St. Mary's Press, 1993). Several autobiographical essays also appear in this collection.

# DAY ONE
## *Climbing Jacob's Ladder*

### *Introducing Our Retreat Theme*

African American spirituality is song-filled, triumphant, confrontational and, above all, mystical. The songs and stories of Sister Thea and Father Bede tell how African American men and women, many (but not all) of whom were enslaved in America, forged an identity and a spirituality out of the Bible and their own African cultural forms. The composers of the body of sacred song known as "The Spirituals" identified with some of the great biblical heroes and focused on passages of Scripture that spoke to the singers' pain, hope, despair and resolution. Some themes are sounded over and over; some biblical figures, like Moses and Jesus, appear frequently in the songs. The music addresses the full range of human concerns and experiences, and in every circumstance both the singer and the listener are pulled into a new way of seeing, a new way of telling an "old, old story."

Through solo and congregational singing, all who experience the rich artistry of African American sacred song are called to "move on up a little higher," in the words of one of Mahalia Jackson's better known recordings. In the earliest compilation of these songs, this theme of moving higher, toward heaven, is found in various texts, from the first, "Roll, Jordan, Roll!" to "The

Old Ship of Zion," which can be found near the end.[1] The idea of a singer (or singers) "climbing Jacob's Ladder," or "wrestling Jacob until the break of day," brings to the fore many of the themes to be explored in this spiritual journey with Sister Thea and Father Bede.

To be actively seeking a place of harmony and peace ("climbing," "moving," "sailing away to heaven"), to be prophetically engaged in bringing important messages from God to fellow believers rooted on earth (only angels—messengers of God, as we read in Genesis 28— traversed the spaces between heaven and earth) is to be caught in a militant mysticism ("soldiers of the Lord") that is a universal theme in the Spirituals.[2]

Often the singers exhort their listeners: "Let's go to God," or "walk together, children," or "come and go with me to that land." So are we invited to share in a journey of reflection and prayer, first to the valley where we "couldn't hear nobody pray," where we "sometimes feel like a motherless child," where "the Jordan river is chilly and cold." Then we will be asked to find in this spirituality the sources of comfort and joy, reminders that "anybody ask you who you are, you tell them you a child of God," that Mary rocked her baby "in a weary land," that even though it is a "deep river," our "home is over Jordan."

Throughout our journey we will be gently and persuasively reminded that when we call God to "come by here," or say to Jesus, "Savior, do not pass me by," our prayers will be answered and we will be led out of the wilderness; we will be reminded that Jesus will lead us, and guide us, and that our journey within and heavenward will be "safe and secure from all alarm," because we will, in the midst of all trials and temptations, be like Thea and Bede, "leaning on the everlasting arm."

We begin in "the valley of the shadow of death," of

Psalm 23, and end on "that great gittin'-up morning." Let us pray for our well-being on the journey. Children, let us pray.

## *Opening Prayer*

Sister Thea and Father Bede, you showed us what it means to be family, as you struggled, day after day, with the storms of life and the troubles of the world. As we set forth to "wade in the water" of prayer, to continue to climb up "the rough side of the mountain," to keep our minds "stayed on Jesus," we ask you to share with us, once again, your songs, your stories, the way you journeyed from pain to bright glory. You never turned back. Help us to keep on keeping on. Lead us, guide us along the way, that we might know the loving kindness of God, a God who has done great things for us, and who will do even greater things, today and tomorrow. For this we pray. Amen.

## *Opening Song*

*I wait upon the Lord, I wait upon the Lord,*
*I wait upon the Lord my God, who take away the sins of the*
    *world.*

*If you want to find Jesus, you have to go in the wilderness,*
*Go in the wilderness, go in the wilderness;*
*If you want to find Jesus, you have to go in the wilderness,*
    *leaning on the Lord.*

*If you want to be a Christian...*

*If you 'spect to be converted...*

*Jesus a-waiting to meet you in the wilderness, meet you in
  the wilderness,*
*Meet you in the wilderness.*
*Jesus a-waiting to meet you in the wilderness, leaning on
  the Lord.*[3]

## Retreat Session One

You will notice the smiles, first of all. Wisdom and
patience and the will to hope beyond all endurance shine
in the faces of Thea Bowman and Bede Abram. Next, you
will notice that, even sitting still, even when pain
overtakes their bodies, as it often did throughout their
lives, they have a restless energy, flickering like fire, that
comes from within and warms those in their presence.

Warm, comforting and completely accepting smiles
greet us as we meet them. We hear Delta sounds in their
voices, which resonate much like the talk of old folks
sitting on porches, late in the evening, giving testimony to
"how they made it over" this day, and countless days
leading up to this one. In their presence we are children
forever, and gratefully so. We can understand the safety
felt by the little children as they sat at the feet of Jesus, as
he taught them that each one of them was more precious
than the sparrows, more "wonderfully and fearfully
made" than the lilies of the field. We listen to the soft,
sweet words and we are drawn into their embrace.

Sister Thea is sitting in a chair, humming quietly to
herself. Soon she begins to sing.

**Thea:**

*When the storms of life are raging, Stand by me.*
*When the storms of life are raging, Stand by me.*
*When the world is tossing me, Like a ship upon the sea;*
*Thou who rulest wind and water, Stand by me.*

*In the midst of tribulations, Stand by me.*
*In the midst of tribulations, Stand by me.*
*When the hosts of hell assail, And my strength begins to*
  *fail,*
*Thou who never lost a battle, Stand by me.*

**Bede:** Sing it, girl. Amen! Let the Church hear it! Amen! We have sure had some raging storms toss us about, haven't we, Thea? All the pain and suffering we had to push through before we could take our blessed rest. Just like the old folks a long time ago. Standing out in cotton fields, or at the bedside of a dying child; or hiding in the woods, where they had run from a whipping. Lord, they knew some raging storms! Can I get a witness? And so did we, and so did we. All we had was a song and some determination and some faith that the Lord was leading us through the storm. When nobody else could feel what we felt, when nobody else knew just how perilous the storm, we had a song.

**Thea:** That is so true, brother Bede. When I used to sit on the steps and listen to the old lady down the street sing to us children, I knew she was telling me a story that couldn't be told any other way. I could hear a lot of crying behind her Hallelujahs, and I always wondered what kind of a storm she had survived. Sing a little of this with me, Bede. You know you just got to moan, you just got to sing sometimes.

**Thea and Bede:**

> *In the midst of faults and failures, Stand by me.*
> *In the midst of faults and failures, Stand by me.*
> *When I do the best I can, and my friends misunderstand,*
> *Thou who knowest all about me, Stand by me.*

**Thea:** You know, Bede, I can remember all the other old folks waving their hands and nodding their heads, and singing along on the last part of the song. And I finally knew just what they meant, those last years and months of my days on earth.

> *When I'm growing old and feeble, Stand by me.*
> *When I'm growing old and feeble, Stand by me.*
> *When my life becomes a burden, And I'm nearing chilly Jordan,*
> *O Thou "Lily of the Valley," Stand by me.*

**Bede:** Amen to that, sister. It is truly a blessed inheritance to claim our black spirituality, especially in times of trouble and heartache. But the joy, Thea, the joy of knowing what our ancestors knew. Because our God is a mighty conqueror, no grave can hold our body down. Even though the Jordan river is "chilly and cold," it can only "chill the body and not the soul."

**Thea:** That's why I kept telling all the children that I was going to live until I died. Because I had been having resurrections from the tomb all my life, I couldn't be afraid of one more death, and one more rising. All those years, Bede, we never taught anything but the old folks' ways, no matter how big the words got sometimes. That's because we knew that we had to link the children of the present times with the ancestors of the days of enslavement if we were to be a family with a future.

**Bede:** And don't forget the ancestors of "way back when." Long before anybody enslaved anybody else and shipped them across the ocean. All the holy men and women from the Bible, and from the days of Jesus, and from the days of the early Church, we had those singing and praying...

**Thea:** And flying....

**Bede:** Ha! That's sure the truth! And flying and preaching and helping Africans adding their spirituality and power to the Hebrew Children and to the early Christian communities. You know, Thea, how happy it made me to discover that the roles of the "Ethiopians" and the "Cushites" and the "Nubians" and the "Cyrenians" in the Scriptures were to be helpers, men and women of great spirituality, integrity, honesty and fortitude. From Jethro and his daughter, Zipporah, keeping Moses safe in Ethiopia, to Ebed-Melech saving Jeremiah's life, all the way up to Simon the Cyrenian helping bear the cross of Jesus along the way, those Africans were there at the crisis time for some mighty important people in the Bible. And you know how my heart was broken to discover that their lives, their backgrounds, their "African-ness" was never ever talked about during all those years I studied theology and Church history.

**Thea:** Of course, I know that. How many times did I hear you starting your lectures and classes by scaring everybody with your introduction to Black Theology:

**Thea and Bede:** "Somebody stole my stuff! Somebody stole my stuff!"

**Thea:** Oh, my brother Bede, we can sit in blessed quiet and rejoice that we found a way out of the darkness of ignorance and confusion concerning who we were and whose we were, but there were some mighty lonesome days for me after I left my mama and daddy's home in Mississippi and journeyed off to meet my life as a woman dedicated to service in the Church.

**Bede:** For me, too. If we had not been taught long and well by the elders and the neighbors and the folks in the community, I don't know if I could have survived it all. I went into the valley and "I couldn't hear nobody pray," at least not in the way I was used to.

**Thea:** From the first day to the last, I made the world hear me when I told my troubles to the Lord.

> Sometimes I feel like a motherless child, sometimes I feel like
>     a motherless child,
> Sometimes I feel like a motherless child, a long ways from
>     home.
> Sometimes I feel like I can't go on, sometimes I feel like I
>     can't go on,
> Sometimes I feel like I can't go on, a long ways from home.

**Bede:** A long ways from home. We chose to follow the gospel, to leave mother and father, sister and brother, and seek the kingdom. God sustained us. Yes, he surely did. He was a rock in a weary land, a shelter from the storm. It was hard for me to talk very much about the loneliness and the sense of distance. I threw myself into whatever was required and kept talking about Jesus as I knew him—even when I must have looked like a complete fool to those around me.

**Thea:** I had no other way, either. Remember those pictures of me in my full Franciscan habit? I was caught up in the rapture of doing the right thing for God because my heart was too full to do anything else. Oh, I kept my hand on the gospel plow. But there were many a day and many a night, when there was none but the Lord to hear my cry. We were a long ways from home....

**Bede:** Except in our hearts. We had our minds stayed on Jesus and we never really lost our way home, not while we had the songs to sing.

**Thea:** Or to moan. Sometimes, all I could do was to hum a song to myself. It would help me fill up many an empty room....

**Bede:** No matter how many people were in it, huh?

**Thea:** That's right. And you know what happened? The song brought folks to me. It was as if my songs were fires, calling people out of the cold of their own particular problems. When I couldn't tell anybody how I felt, I could sing, or hum, or moan a little of my heart, and I felt better. And others seemed to feel better.

**Bede:** That started in the bottom of slave ships, when somebody, in a darkness darker than the blackest midnight, groaned her pain in the anonymous forever-night of the middle passage. When somebody chained to somebody else answered that groan, our spirituality was born. Two souls joined together in the lowest pit of hell started to climb back up to their humanity.

**Thea:** Oh, yes, Bede. Oh, yes, yes, yes. We lived it all, we carry the history of our people, and their transcending faith, within our memories, within our own stories. No matter how rough the journey, and how lonely the walk, we found somebody to hear us, in the night season and all the day long. We heard somebody bend down his head and hear us. And we could keep our eyes on the cross, and use it as our compass to take us out of the valley and guide us along the highway to heaven.

**Bede:** We were climbing Jacob's ladder, just like the angels who visited the earth in time of dreams. We dreamed and sang ourselves along the way.

**Thea:** Because the old folks taught us how to pray with everything we had.

**Bede:** And they taught us how to get more if we needed it. I'm so glad Jesus lifted me.

**Thea:** Singing "Glory! Hallelujah! Jesus lifted me."

## *For Reflection*

- *Reflect on a period of your life when you experienced strong feelings of alienation and loneliness. As you remember these feelings, begin a prayer to God, expressing your need for connection. When you have finished your prayer, try humming a favorite hymn, letting the song touch the alienation and loneliness.*

- *Select a passage of Scripture that involves a favorite character. In what ways do you identify with this scriptural character? Try to take on that person's qualities and virtues as you try to make sense of some of your situations and conditions of confusion and need.*

- *As part of your own sense of connectedness to your "ancestors in the faith," are you comfortable telling stories about the women and men who helped to teach you what it means to be a believer? In a notebook kept for this retreat, write down one or two such memories as a "spiritual photo album." Offer a prayer of thanksgiving to your "ancestors in faith" for the gifts they brought forth in you.*

■ *What are some of the circumstances in your present life that you would name as "valleys" and "deserts"? Invite Jesus to dwell with you where you are.*

## Closing Prayer

### Psalm 23

The LORD is my shepherd, I shall not want.
He makes me lie down in green pastures;
he leads me beside still waters;
    he restores my soul.
He leads me in right paths for his name's sake.

Even though I walk through the darkest valley,
    I fear no evil;
for you are with me;
    your rod and your staff—they comfort me.

You prepare a table before me
 in the presence of my enemies;
you anoint my head with oil;
    my cup overflows.
Surely goodness and mercy shall follow me
    all the days of my life,
and I shall dwell in the house of the LORD
    my whole life long.

## Closing Song

*When the storms of life are raging, Stand by me.*
*When the storms of life are raging, Stand by me.*
*When the world is tossing me, Like a ship upon the sea;*
*Thou who rulest wind and water, Stand by me.*

*In the midst of tribulations, Stand by me.*
*In the midst of tribulations, Stand by me.*
*When the hosts of hell assail, And my strength begins to*
   *fail,*
*Thou who never lost a battle, Stand by me.*

*In the midst of faults and failures, Stand by me.*
*In the midst of faults and failures, Stand by me.*
*When I do the best I can, And my friends misunderstand,*
*Thou who knowest all about me, Stand by me.*

## Notes

[1] These songs, compiled in 1867 by William Francis Allen, Charles P. Ware and Lucy McKim Garrison, in the important collection, *Slave Songs of the United States,* have been reissued by Dover Publications, Mineola, New York (1995). Other collections of songs will be found in the section, *Deepening Your Acquaintance,* at the end of this book.

[2] Throughout this book, I have made an extreme effort to standardize the spellings of words that might appear in dialect in older versions of the Spirituals. For decades it has been my observation that dialect-typography is often used to distance the reader from the content of the work, and not to highlight the creative genius of the artists being studied. Human beings do not write their native languages in dialect. With regard to the transcription of African American speech, the use of dialect is, in my thinking, most often due to a confusion between regional accents and the inability of the transcriber to accurately put onto paper the intricacies of an inflected speech. Stereotypical "black dialect" was and continues to be a mask, sometimes imposed upon the performer by the audience, sometimes assumed by the performer to add elements of irony and distance to the material being shared. In other words, what we see and what we hear are often two different

languages. Whenever possible, I have opted to make the seeing consistent.

[3] "Go in the Wilderness," performed by the Princely Players (*Wade in the Water*, Volume I: *African American Spirituals: The Concert Tradition*. Smithsonian Folkways Record, SF 40072).

# Day Two
## Wading in the Water

### Coming Together in the Spirit

The spirituality we are embracing in this retreat is, in the words of the African American Catholic bishops (in their pastoral letter, *What We Have Seen and Heard*), "authentically black and truly Catholic."[1] The elements of African American spirituality used here are gathered from the centuries of specific cultural experiences shared by millions of individuals who were unwilling immigrants, victims of the horrific "middle passage." The trade in human oppression moved from the western coast of Africa into the ports of Spanish and Portugese America and into the English and Dutch (and Danish and Swedish) territories of the Americas. The men and women of Africa, mostly.young and always healthy, were penned in the holds of the slaving ships and journeyed, on many levels, in the "middle" of a hellish translocation. Because of heroic choices of survival they made of themselves a people, nations within nations. They forged an identity and a faith based on their African heritages and the messages of deliverance they extracted from forms of Christianity that were often used to keep them confused, alienated and hopeless.[2]

Certain biblical themes and particular scriptural and historical figures are often employed in the songs, stories and sermons which are the foundations of African American spirituality. These themes and figures are often taken from the stories of bondage, exile and abandonment found in the Old Testament. Familiar themes of the New Testament are employed over and over in the songs and sermons, and deal mostly with the nature of Jesus as Suffering Servant, faithful Child of God and triumphant Lamb upon the Throne of Revelation.

No matter how bleak the dramatic setting, the theme of the songs and prayers of African American Christians is almost always the same: surviving the storm. Calling on Jesus to still the raging sea, the great singers and prophets, the humble servants and friends of the Savior are always confident that God will hear their cry and deliver them. Our starting point is this question: What makes the spirituality of African Americans so compelling to so many fellow believers of every country and culture? The raging sea, the burning desert, the "friendless world," the "weary land" are pictured and evoked with the artistry of genius, and all who experience the articulations of this spirituality are drawn in, body and spirit, to remember or recognize their own particular wilderness. This bond makes the songs of deliverance that much sweeter to sing and to hear.


## *Opening Song*

### "Kum Ba Yah" (Come By Here)

*Kum ba yah, my Lord, Kum ba yah,*
*Kum ba yah, my Lord, Kum ba yah,*
*Kum ba yah, my Lord, Kum ba yah,*
*Oh, Lord, Kum ba yah.*

*Someone's crying, Lord, Kum ba yah,*

*Someone's crying, Lord, Kum ba yah,*
*Someone's crying, Lord, Kum ba yah,*
*Oh, Lord, Kum ba yah.*

*Someone's singing, Lord, Kum ba yah....*
*Someone's praying, Lord, Kum ba yah....*
*Someone needs you, Lord, Kum ba yah....*[3]

### *Opening Prayer*

Dear Lord, when we remember those who have gone before us, marked in the sign of faith, and sealed in the Blood of the Lamb, we see ourselves often as small and frightened and alone. We stretch out our hands to you, O God, and we open our hearts to your life-giving Spirit. Help us to see that we are as precious in your sight as the mightiest of your angels, and show us, once again, that you care for us and pour out your love for us, knowing us by name in our mother's womb, and hearing us whenever we call to you. Let your perfect love dispel the darkness and fear that sometimes paralyze us, and make our feet to sometimes falter. We are your children and we hope in thee. Amen.

# RETREAT SESSION TWO

**Thea:** "Looking for a blessing, Lord, Come by here, Looking for blessing, Lord, Come by here...."

**Bede:** The old folks who came up with that song sure had a mighty strong faith, didn't they, Thea? I mean, think about it. They had been told and told and told that they were put on this earth to serve a human master, that God made them to pick up after a human mistress, that they were to be obedient and humble and quiet and quick. Some even got told that they were going to be slaves even when they got to heaven.

**Thea:** And they would sneak off to the trees beyond the fields, late at night, after they were so bone-weary from work that they could hardly swallow their own spit, and they would find some spot, covered over with dense trees and vines, and they would kneel down in the dirt, and tell God that they knew the truth from a lie: that any God who could deliver *some* folks from slavery could deliver *all folks* from oppression. And that's why we can sing this song, today, anywhere and in any way we want to. 'Cause, you don't need to be an actual in-chains slave to know how small you can feel sometimes. And you don't have to run away to the woods to understand that sometimes all you can do is hope God will hear you in the midst of your turmoil....

**Bede:** And the trouble of the world.

**Thea:** Amen. And the trouble of the world. They knew they couldn't run from the trouble, but they certainly did believe that God could be with them, even there.

**Bede:** Especially there. Long after the days of "so-called freedom," the old folks still found some quiet place to call on the Lord. It could have been a rocking chair in the bedroom, or a stool on the back porch. When the troubles got to them, they would start to moan, or hum, and that would start the calling-down of God.

**Thea:** They knew that God would hear them, because they had heard a lot more of the Bible than just "slaves obey your masters." They knew that "the prayers of the righteous availeth much." They knew that "His eye is on the sparrow," and that he watches over us all. They learned fast and they learned well. A little talk with Jesus makes it right.

**Bede:** When people today talk about "centering prayer," or when I hear other guides talk about "composition of place," or finding a mystical connectedness in one's prayer, I can think of my own grandmother and granddaddy, sitting in their rooms at night, with the smell of life on them. Racism. Discrimination. Misunderstanding. A harsh or unfeeling word hurled at their souls. Not knowing how to pay the rent. Finding out that the eldest child was picked up by the police. And they would sit there, in their chairs at night. And because she couldn't speak the "King's English," and also because the pain was so great sometimes she couldn't articulate it, she would sit in her chair, and her body would start swaying. And she would say, "humm, humm, humm." And with the smell of life on her, as she "sat in the garden alone, with the dew still on the roses," her moan simply said, "sometimes I feel like a motherless child," "nobody knows the trouble I've seen...hmmm." "I'm gonna have a little talk with Jesus, tell him all my troubles."

And in that moment, God made himself known. In that moment, my grandmother, my grandfather, were caught up in the encounter with God.

**Thea:** In that moment, he "walked with her, and he talked with her, and he told her she was his own." And after that moment, your grandmama and your granddaddy could get out of that chair, go back into the living room and tell the children, "Don't you all worry about a thing. God is on our side."

**Bede:** That's what the covenant meant to them, and what it ought to mean to us. Our ancestors stood on the banks of the Jordan River, this time called *America*, and saw a multitude of powerful people proclaiming themselves to be God-fearing, covenant-swearing, chosen people. Our ancestors stood on the wayside, often not allowed to traverse the same highways as their masters and mistresses. Like the blind man in the Bible, they stood on the side of the road, and they cried....

**Thea:** And they sang, "Come by here, my Lord, come by here."

**Bede:** "Kum ba yah, my Lord, kum ba yah."

**Thea:** These old folks we're talking about, Brother Bede, made up their minds that if they could see themselves to be a new manifestation of the Children of Israel, caught up in a new Egypt, bound and oppressed by all sorts of new Pharaohs, then the old Delivering Jehovah they heard about....

**Bede:** Or sneaked off and learned to read about. Amen.

**Thea:** Amen. Or read about, and talked about—well, if that God could deliver Daniel, then why not every blessed child among them? So they let the whispering of their heart-moans escape their lips. "Kum ba yah," they said. And when they cried upon the Lord, just like the children of Abraham caught up in making bricks out of straw for Pharaoh, they were choosing this God to be their God.

**Bede:** From the very beginning they worked for their freedom by replacing the ground that had been snatched from under their feet with the holy ground of the Bible. They looked over some dinky little stream in Alabama and saw the Jordan, instead.

**Thea:** And they looked at their friends and neighbors dressed up in clean rags, or clothes cast off from the Big House, and instead of seeing a brother, a sister, an aunt or uncle, they saw a "band all dressed in red," and decided that who they saw, in the eyes of mystical faith, were really "the band that Moses led." They got down to the creekbed and looked at everybody getting ready for a secret baptism, and declared, "see that band all dressed in white, looks like the children of the Israelites."

**Bede:** That's the real meaning of "liberation" in liberation theology, for me. These men and women, learning a new language and a new way of existing, picked up the religion that obviously seemed to be working for those who oppressed them, and forged a relationship with the God of their "enemies," and in the process connected themselves with a hope and a faith that we can only marvel at today. God found Moses in the desert and lit up the burning bush. Because God had heard the cry of the suffering children of Jacob. The old folks we are talking about lit up a bush of faith, and made it a beacon burning to get this same God's attention. God said to Moses, "Come up here." The cast-off old folks said to God, "Kum ba yah."

**Thea:** The songs they sang became as holy and as sacred as the psalms of David.

**Bede:** These songs are the psalms of a new people, holy, consecrated, a people set apart. And anybody in need can sing these songs, and get the same comfort from them as the original singers got. Just as we sit down in church and pray the psalms. Only, most of the time, we don't have to step over all the ones about dashing our enemies' brains out and hacking them to pieces.

**Thea:** Oh, Bede, ain't it the truth? The old folks in the family were a lot more forgiving of their oppressors than you can almost ever find the psalm singers being in the Bible. I sometimes wonder if any of us nowadays can ever understand the powerful spirituality they possessed. To be able to call God for their deliverance from bondage, and to still say, "He's got the whole world in his hands." Were they the ignorant, naive, brainwashed children a lot of people call them?

**Bede:** Now, Thea, you know one of my favorite songs gets right to the heart of that problem:

> *Everybody talking 'bout heaven ain't going there. Heaven.*
> *Heaven.*
> *Gonna' walk all over God's heaven.*

They knew that it was only by righteous living and acting, putting the implications of the covenant into practice, that they would get their heavenly—and earthly—reward.

**Thea:** Oh, I know, Bede. It's just that sometimes I get so humble in the face of their overwhelming faith. They made a covenant with God, in the harshest of circumstances, in the most horrible of existences. They kept their minds and hearts "stayed on Jesus," and they never gave up hoping and working for their deliverance. They did not wait for Moses to lead them all out at once.

One by one, two by two, they would "steal away to Jesus," and keep on stealing away until they got to Buffalo. Their covenant with God gave them a meaning and a method. There might have been many a Moses among the more courageous women and men, like Harriet Tubman. But the covenant was written upon hearts of flesh, just like Ezekiel prophesied it would be. And they could see through the rhetoric of "lip-service Christians," and know that righteous behavior was the single most important consequence of entering into a covenant with God.

**Bede:** And that understanding gave them the courage to "wade in the water," didn't it? Once they saw themselves as children of the Israelite, as the band that Moses led, once they saw themselves as able to enter into a relationship with a God who was both merciful and just, then they could step on off into fully living. Even if that meant walking into dangers that could kill them.

**Thea:** The Jordan River is chilly and cold. It chills the body...but not the soul.

**Bede:** Especially if the "soul's been anchored in the Lord." The old folks had discerning minds and hearts. Wiser than Solomon, when it came to seeing the hand of God in the midst of a sea of trouble. Some part of our inheritance is being lost when we lose our ability to savor the old songs. We learned them because they were everywhere in our environment. They were a part of our day, like air, or rain, or sunshine. Somebody was always singing, somewhere.

**Thea:** That was the way I found the music all over Africa when I visited there. Drummers and singers, and music-making all along the side of the road, on the buses, in public buildings. Everywhere. Folks brought the understanding with them. No matter where you find yourself, no matter what problem you suddenly encounter, you can start a song. And you can change reality in the space of a breath. The songs of our people are the key to understanding our faith.

**Bede:** While we are thinking about "Wade in the Water," we ought to remember some water that chilled body and soul, and cut off the life of many a poor motherless child—the Atlantic during the period called the "middle passage." Nobody knows how many millions of mamas and daddies, baby sons and daughters, proud and beautiful young men and women got shoved into the midnight bellies of those stinking ships, and who never saw the light again. Nobody can ever count the graves lost beneath the ocean. But even in the hold of those ships, even in the pits of the holding pens along the African coast, there were encounters with a transcendent force that is part of our legacy.

**Thea:** That's right. When those poor abused children of God were shuffled together like a deck of cards, or were stirred together as close as grains of rice, when the darkness of the night matched the darkness of their condition, somebody cried out and wept and moaned and sighed.

**Bede:** And somebody else, a somebody else who couldn't even speak the language of the first suffering lost child, added her groaning voice to the crying and weeping around her. And another somebody else put his sorrow into the sweltering air. And somebody else and somebody else just lay there, stretched out in pain and crippling grief, held fast in cold chains, and listened and knew he was not alone.

**Thea:** And in the groaning, in the sighing, in the bitterest pain, they forged their voices together in order to hold their souls bound, at least for that one endless night. And it was a prayer. And a song. And a calling down of a power that had no name, to still the terror. Just for a little bit.

**Bede:** Oh, Thea! How we need to remember what they learned then. How we need to remember that God is found wherever we find ourselves. Those that found a way to swallow the terror and turn it into a reaching out to somebody else in the darkness—how profound, how full of grace they were.

**Thea:** This is the wisdom locked into our song. "Wade in the water, children. Wade in the water. *God's* gonna trouble the water." You see, I take that to mean that if you can have the faith to understand—even at time of the greatest panic—that upheavals and catastrophes, tragedies and destruction can be stood up to, and can be withstood, if you hold on to what might be the slenderest thread of faith imaginable, then you don't have to drown. Our ancestors were not some group of silly, unthinking dupes who looked for God to keep them out of trouble. No, bless God! They knew that if you step in the water, it is going to roil and splash. They knew that there was no way to avoid the flood. They just knew what only a survivor can tell you. Some trouble can be overcome. And trouble don't last always.

**Bede:** Now, girl, you just slipped into the neighborhood of the blues. "I know the sun's gonna shine in my back door some day."

**Thea:** The "blues" and the "Spirituals" are the same song with different words—even that sometimes. When you just got to shout out, "Have Mercy!" And some stranger walking by says, "Amen! Brother!" then you are in the realm of the holy and the wonderful. But it is the trouble that is the starting point. You can't curse and pray at the same time. And you can't stay in the middle of hell when you are singing about flying away to be at rest. You can feel like the worst abandoned motherless child, and as soon as you hear some old lady singing about her Jesus while she's cleaning greens for supper, then you know you belong somewhere, to somebody, and you know you got a home to get to, some day. As you step on past that kitchen window, your walk is going to naturally have more grace to it.

**Bede:** That's why the song says, "Wade in the water, children." Wade. Don't float, or flounder, or swamp yourself or drown. Wade. We have to remember how much biblical theology the old folks knew. This song squeezes so much salvation history into one single line, that some people might miss all of it....

**Thea:** And think it's some cute little song to sing at summer camp. And nothing more. Whenever I taught the children to sing this song, and a whole lot more of them, I would tell what each song was about. They could sing it better then.

**Bede:** Oh, yes, we have to know about all sorts of water when we sing this. And how to get into it right, so we can get out of it whole. You know they were seeing the Hebrew children, standing there at the edge of the Red Sea looking at all that water, every once in a while glancing back and seeing all that sand being raised by Pharaoh's chariots and horses. Oh, they saw some trouble, behind them and before. And they hadn't been all that sold on Moses, nohow. All his fancy tricks with snakes and frogs and darkness got forgotten real quick when they could smell the salt before them and taste the sand blowing at their backs.

**Thea:** You working this one, Bede. And so what did they do?

**Bede:** They grumbled. They forgot the Passover, just that fast. And they looked real sour at Moses and said, "We can't go on and we can't turn back. Now what this God of yours going to do?" And the old folks say Moses said:

> *Wade in the water; wade in the water, children;*
> *wade in the water, God's gonna trouble the water.*

And they did. They learned the first lesson of deliverance. We must be delivered from our fear. Not all the trouble of the world is unto death. Sometimes God stirs up our lives so that we can get out of danger, and into a new place, with a whole *lot* more life in it. Maybe they had to sing something the whole time they walked through the walls of sea, just to keep their conviction as strong as the mountains of water hovering over them. They marched and they sang. And they made it over to the other side. What?

**Thea:** I was just thinking of the other "God-troubled" water that the old folks must have been singing about in this song. The beautiful pool in John's Gospel.

> Now in Jerusalem by the Sheep Gate there is a pool,
> called in Hebrew Beth-zatha, which has five
> porticoes. In these lay many invalids, blind, lame,
> and paralyzed. One man was there who had been ill

47

for thirty-eight years. When Jesus saw him lying there and that he had been there a long time, he said to him, "Do you want to be made well?" The sick man answered him, "Sir, I have no one to put me into the pool when the water is stirred up; and while I am making my way, someone else steps down ahead of me." Jesus said to him, "Stand up, take your mat and walk." And at once the man was made well, and he took up his mat and began to walk. (John 5:2-9)

**Bede:** That is what it is all about, what it has always been about. "Do you want to be healed?" My Lord! What a morning! To lay there, all those years, seeing others push past you, greedy for a healing power to transform them, oblivious to your pain and suffering. "Do you want to be healed?" That's why they could moan their assent to this story, and tell this God with the power to heal to "come by here." The old singers and praying ancestors learned the scriptural lesson very well, indeed. They wanted to be in the water when the angel of God "troubled" it. From a distance, from the shore or from the temple balcony, trouble just looks like trouble. When you are deep in the midst of it, when you've been carrying it or have been weighed down—paralyzed by trouble for days, weeks, months, for years—then you know that the change that God will bring to your life is radically different from whatever it is you have been enduring. Change. Freedom. Restoration. A new perspective. A new way of doing things. The ability to get up and walk away from the crippling fear and worrying anxieties and doubts. Only somebody who had been able to experience the change brought about by God's redeeming grace could speak with the authority of Jesus.

**Thea:** He said, "Rise...and walk." They said, "Wade in the water." God said to the Hebrew children, "Eat standing up, because you've got to be ready to pass over from slavery to freedom." And the old folks keep on singing, "My soul looks back in wonder at how I made it over." And, Bede, you know, even when you can't sing the songs, you can feel them. They make you want to sway your body, and dip your shoulders, and you just naturally get a smile on your face, and your throat relaxes, and your hands can lay peaceful in your lap. Sometimes when the pain got so bad in my life it felt like I was being turned inside out like you would pull off a glove, I could hear a song in my head, and I could hold on to the song for just a little rest. I like to think it was God troubling the water.

**Bede:** It surely is that, Thea. It surely is.

**Thea:** Jesus is a rock in a weary land. A shelter in a time of storm. But the weariness was in the land when they got to it, and the storm was raging long before they could say the Savior's sweet, sweet name. They were looking for a blessing. They were standing in the need of prayer. When God heard their prayer, they were able to build themselves a harbor, where the Old Ship of Zion could safely rest. When they stole away to the brush arbors and whispered out the pain of their souls, the burden lifted because they knew that "Jesus did just what he said, he healed the sick and he raised the dead."

**Bede:** The ancient covenant was made new in the lives and songs of the old folks. When God "came by them," they grabbed God's almighty and healing hand, and held on for dear life.

**Thea:** And so did we, Bede, so did we.

## For Reflection

- *Where are the places in your life today that make you feel overwhelmed with anxiety, fear and trouble? In what ways have you attempted to ask for healing?*

- *Are there circumstances in your life with which you can identify with the paralyzed person caught at the Bethesda pool? How might you minister to others who have been unable to "enter the pool"?*

- *What are the blessings in your life that seem most important to you as you share in this meditation? In what ways do you think God has heard you when you called, "Come by here"?*

## Closing Prayer

O God, you have been a shelter in the storms of our lives, you have been a refuge and a place of safety for me when I have felt most lost, abandoned and alone. In the depths of my sorrow and anguish, I have felt your gentle touch and your healing power. Once again, I ask you to be with me and send the light of heaven into my soul. Burn away my doubts and my anxiety in the face of the turmoil of my world, and grant me peace in all my endeavors. Let me hear your voice in the stillness after the whirlwinds of my daily distractions and concerns. Teach me your paths, O Lord, that we might walk together in the garden as friends. Amen.

## Closing Song

*Father, I stretch my hands to Thee, No other help I know;*

*If Thou withdraw Thyself from me, Ah! whither shall I go?*

*What did Thine only Son endure, Before I drew my breath!*
*What pain, what labor to secure My soul from endless*
*death!*

*Surely Thou canst not let me die, O speak and I shall live;*
*And here I will unwearied lie, Till Thou Thy spirit give.*

*Author of faith! to Thee I lift My weary, longing eyes:*
*O let me now receive that gift! My soul without it dies.*[4]

## Notes

[1] *What We Have Seen and Heard: A Pastoral Letter on Evangelization From the Black Bishops of the United States* (Cincinnati, Ohio: St. Anthony Messenger Press, 1984), p. 30.

[2] Of the many studies of the "middle passage," two are especially inspiring. Vincent Franklin offers an understanding of the "choice for survival," in *There is a River: The Black Struggle for Freedom in America* (New York: Vintage Books, 1981). The facts and features of the middle passage are easily available in *Black Saga: The African American Experience* (Boston: Houghton Mifflin, 1995), by Charles M. Christian. Both of these texts will lead the reader to further sources.

[3] As found in *Songs of Zion* (Nashville, Tenn.: Abingdon Press, 1982), #139. A version, with modernized spelling, can be found in *Lead Me, Guide Me: The African American Catholic Hymnal* (Chicago: G.I.A. Publications, 1987), #218.

[4] *Lead Me, Guide Me*, #223. This is one of the most powerful of the Spirituals, still chanted in black churches throughout the United States, in a call-and-response rendition that is virtually unchanged from the days of enslavement.

# DAY THREE
## Trying on Our Wings

### Coming Together in the Spirit

In *Say Amen, Somebody*, the great documentary on traditional gospel music and its pioneers, Mother Willie Mae Ford Smith, the singing evangelist from St. Louis, Missouri, is given pride of place.[1] Much of the film deals with a celebration in honor of Mother Smith, focusing on her family, her colleagues and those for whom she served as mentor in the field of gospel music evangelism. In the beginning, Mother Smith is seen visiting a local nursing home, where she sings some of her most popular songs while accompanied by her eldest child, Bertha. Eventually, as the camera pulls back, the viewer can see that Mother Smith must use an aluminum walker to get about. In most of the other scenes involving Willie Mae Ford Smith, she is photographed either sitting or standing still.

At the end of the movie, after a host of Mother Smith's "children" (both biological and "in the spirit") have performed, she herself takes the stage. During the performance of one of her classic songs, "Canaan," Mother Willie Mae Ford Smith "moves out" in a moment when she is captured by the spirit of the song. She steps down to sing to the congregation, pointing to each of her own children and testifying to all those near her. As she sings and gestures and steps among those gathered, the camera again pulls back. This time, we see that Mother Smith is moving without the aid of the walker. Her grandson accompanies her, but it is obvious that he is next to her for the sheer formality of offering her his aid if she should need it. Lifted up with the sentiments of the song, she doesn't need him. One of her most famous recordings asks, "give me wings, Lord...wings of faith, that I might fly away and be at rest." In the closing moments of *Say Amen, Somebody*, Willie Mae Ford Smith shows the viewer just how real those wings can be.

## *Defining Our Thematic Context*

In her introduction to the African American Catholic hymnal, *Lead Me, Guide Me*, Sister Thea Bowman makes the following astute observation: "The singer lifts the Church, the people, to a higher level of understanding, feeling, motivation, and participation."[2] All those who offer commentary and understanding of how black sacred song is used, privately and liturgically, are unanimous in their agreement with this insight. When a singer, be it in church or on some electronic device, "gets down" with the music, the listener is transported to another realm. This is not an accidental side-effect of the performance. For the musicians who compose and present black sacred song, it is their intention to put all who hear the song "way up in the middle of the air" so that we, too, can view the heavenly host and see Ezekiel's wheels turning around every which way.

Thea Bowman, a singer of grace and genius herself, could understand the dynamic employed in the offering of the song. In the just-quoted introduction, she also says:

The singer is chosen from the people by the people

to suit their immediate need.

> *"Sometimes I feel like a motherless child."*
> *"I just came from the fountain."*
> *"I love the Lord."*
> *"My Heavenly Father watches over me."*

The first person pronoun, the "I" reference is communal. The individual sings the soul of the community. In heart and voice and gesture the Church, the community responds.

What she says of black sacred music can be seen in the lyric content of many of the old Spirituals and of many of the "traditional" gospel songs. "Give me wings, Lord." "I know my wings are gonna fit me well. I tried them on at the Gates of Hell." "I, John, saw the Holy Number, the zig-zag lightning and the rolling thunder." And on and on. The composer/singer/performer established a flash of mystical awareness in each rendition of these and other songs. When the singer "gets happy," no listener can remain unaffected. This ecstatic performance, "in heart and voice and gesture," is, perhaps surprisingly, one of the intersecting moments where traditional African and classic Christian European forms of prayer are found still connected. When one sings, "O, sister, you ought to been there/ a sitting in the Kingdom/ just to hear sweet Jordan roll," the vision is no different from the many recorded by and about such great mystics as John of the Cross, or Teresa of Avila. For instance, Saint Teresa says in her *Autobiography*, "The cloud ascends to heaven and brings the soul along, and begins to show it the things of the kingdom that He prepared for it."[3] John of the Cross makes this comment on the soul being in the presence of God:

> The soul now feels that it is all inflamed in the divine union and that its palate is all bathed in glory and

love, that in the most intimate part of its substance it
is flooded with no less than rivers of glory,
abounding in delights, and that from its bosom flow
rivers of living water...which the Son of God declared
will rise up in such souls. Accordingly it seems,
because the soul is so vigorously transformed in
God, so sublimely possessed by Him, and arrayed
with such rich gifts and virtues, that it is singularly
close to beatitude—so close that only a thin veil
separates it.[4]

As any who study the mysticism of the Renaissance will
attest, it is the general teaching that the taste of the future
fullness of the resurrected body has been reserved to the
few who have been called mystics in the European
Catholic and Christian traditions.

In the African American Christian (and therefore,
Catholic) traditions of prayer, mystical transport is the
expected outcome of singing the sacred songs. It is a
"truly catholic" expectation, in that it is the expectation of
all that when the church service is over, everyone within
hearing or shouting range can say, "I just came from the
fountain." Once again it is important to emphasize that
the ecstatic tradition being considered here is communal
and participatory. The songs transport and transform us.
We do not have to contemplate how we must strive to find
the unitive way, as would those who learn of mysticism
from the writings of the great Renaissance saints. We need
only turn ourselves over to the dynamic of the song in
order to find ourselves possessed by the Spirit. "The
singer is chosen from the people by the people to suit their
immediate need," Sister Thea says. We understand that
when one is at the very gates of hell, a song that can lift
you up and carry you to safety is a very strong spiritual
aid.

## Opening Song

*Ev'ry Time I Feel the Spirit moving in my heart,*
*I will pray.*
*Ev'ry Time I Feel the Spirit moving in my heart,*
*I will pray.*

*Upon the mountain my Lord spoke, Out His mouth*
*came fire and smoke.*
*All around me looks so shine, Asked the Lord if all*
*was mine.*

*Ev'ry Time I Feel the Spirit moving in my heart,*
*I will pray.*
*Ev'ry Time I Feel the Spirit moving in my heart,*
*I will pray.*

*Jordan river is chilly and cold, Chills the body but*
*not the soul.*
*Ain't but one train on this track, Runs to heaven*
*and runs right back.*

*Ev'ry Time I Feel the Spirit moving in my heart,*
*I will pray.*
*Ev'ry Time I Feel the Spirit moving in my heart,*
*I will pray.*

## Opening Prayer

Holy Spirit of God, open us to the power of your transforming fire. Where we are in doubt, fill us with the certainty of faith. Where we are weary, quicken us with your power. Where we feel oppressed on all sides, carry us to safety and keep us from all harm. Amen.

# RETREAT SESSION THREE

**Bede:** Thea, let me ask you something. I have known you forever and ever, and whenever I heard you sing, even in the days of all that painful radiation therapy, and in those moments when you had the feverish aching and almost unendurable pain in your bones, whenever I heard you sing, I could sense that you left the pain "somewhere else" while you were singing. Am I right? And how did you do it?

**Thea:** Oh, yes, my brother, I could leave the pain for just a little while. Until I couldn't travel any more, and had to stay in that bed until the end, I was able to find some spark within and nurture it long enough with song that the flame could hold the pain at bay. How did I do it? I don't think *I* did it, Bede. I believe, more and more, that the old folks put some sort of healing into the songs, and taught us how to sing them for more than only the praise of God. I think we have songs of faith that could live up to the injunction of Jesus:

> If you had faith the size of a mustard seed, you could say to this mulberry tree, "Be uprooted, and planted in the sea," and it would obey you (Luke 17:6).

Think about the men and women, some of them as old as old could be, who would spend hours of the night performing a "ring-shout." After a prayer service was over in the church they would go outside, some of them, and sing and testify and dance until it was practically dawn and time for them to go back to the fields or to the big house and start their earthly toil all over again. With no sleep they were able to work as refreshed as if they had spent the night in slumber. Yet they had been dancing in a counter-clockwise circle for five or six hours, all the while singing until they were in a trance.

**Bede:** How do you think the trance came about? I think it was due to the way they kept the drums alive, after they were punished for using them. I know how the drumming all over Africa, and in the West Indies and in Latin America led to all sorts of Afro-Christian religious practices such as *Candomblè* and *Santeria* and *Vodou*, and I have become convinced that when the people who practice those variations on African worship styles get "possessed," it sure looks a lot like some Baptist folks in Alabama getting happy in church.

**Thea:** And not only Baptists, but many, many others, and that includes a few Catholics nowadays. And we both know that ability to shout and get possessed by the Spirit is not restricted to members of any ethnic group. I think you are right, Bede, about the drum-induced trance. You know how the style of repetition plays such an important role in black sacred song, both the oldest music and the most contemporary. Singing the same phrase over and over is a form of self-hypnosis—no different from a Buddhist mantra.

**Bede:** Or reciting all fifteen mysteries of the rosary. Or repeating, "Lord Jesus, have mercy on me, a sinner," or any number of other forms of repetitive prayer. Each of those forms can alter the breathing of the one doing the praying and bring about a changed state of awareness. Oh, yes, Thea, I'm with you on this one. Rhythmically moving in a circle, stamping the feet and clapping one's hands—all the while singing a phrase of music over and over again—yes, that could take your mind to a different level of awareness.

**Thea:** And the dynamic will work, no matter what the lyric is. Which is why some folks get so upset with some of the popular music of the day. And why the young folks hold on to that music so hard and fast. It does make them feel "different," maybe *better*, maybe not. But the right rhythm and the repetition of a phrase or two, over and over, will induce a visionary state as often as not.

**Bede:** So, what you are saying is, the use we put the music to will determine where the music takes us.

**Thea:** I'm saying that, and a whole lot more, Bede. I'm saying that the wisest of the old singers/composers/performers devised messages in the music, and planted solutions to problems in the music—and those messages and solutions still have a high worth today.

**Bede:** For instance?

**Thea:** For instance, all the songs that have to do with praise, with flying, with marching, with moving, with seeing heaven. And I think I would include on this list quite a few of the songs that ask for healing and mercy. Now—and this is very important to my way of looking at these songs—most of the songs I am talking about start out real slow when you sing them and can be picked up in speed as you go along. They pull you into the rhythm, and then you get caught up, until you can't escape the experience. And if a person doesn't know how to surrender to the rhythm, it can be a very scary experience indeed.

**Bede:** That's another truth you just told. I am reminded of just how terrified Du Bois got when he walked into one of those all-night ring-shouts out in the darkness of rural Tennessee one summer while he was teaching as part of his undergraduate requirements.

> The people moaned and fluttered, and then the gaunt-cheeked brown woman beside me suddenly leaped straight into the air and shrieked like a lost soul, while round about came wail and groan and outcry, and a scene of human passion such as I had never conceived before.[5]

**Thea:** My Sweet Jesus! He sure was an Episcopalian from Massachusetts, wasn't he? Wonder what he would have made of some of the services where we sang and preached, huh, Bede? But Dr. Du Bois did understand the deep-rooted spirituality in the midst of the "frenzy," as he called it later on. He knew he was in the middle of something profoundly holy and awe-inspiring. And we have learned to respect the same tradition, and we have had the good fortune to study at length what he stumbled upon that night.

What they were doing was calling down the Spirit of God to consume them and change them, to fortify them and sustain them. It was not a hunger to "leave the world," as some would say in criticism. No, it was a determination to be so transformed by the Spirit that the world could not touch them with its evil, madness and soul-destruction.

**Bede:** The spirituality they employed also had a root in something we have already talked about: identification with the heroes of the Bible. In the other variations on this African tradition of spirit possession, these old Christians picked some powerful folks from the Bible, studied their lives and their actions and set out to become possessed of the virtues and qualities as found in the great figures of salvation history.

**Thea:** Like Moses, and Daniel and David, and Mary and Martha. And Peter, John and Paul. The woman at the well, the blind man who stood on the side of the road and a whole passel of suffering women and children. One really sharp example of "putting on the wings of faith" and becoming caught up in one of the stories of the Bible to the point where the singers act out the story is "Joshua fit the battle of Jericho."

**Bede:** I know it must be one of your favorites. I remember how you used to sing it, making it sound as if the walls really were falling down, just by the way you would make your voice swoop and tumble and crash. You used to have some real fun singing that song.

**Thea:** You can get a child to remember anything if you make the learning fun. The lessons in the song are grown-up lessons, but the fun ain't never had an age limit as far as I am concerned.

**Bede:** Amen. Let's sing it now, Thea.

> *Joshua fit the battle of Jericho, Jericho, Jericho;*
> *Joshua fit the battle of Jericho, and the walls come tumbling down.*
> *You may talk about your king of Gideon, you make talk about your man of Saul,*
> *There's none like good old Joshua, At the battle of Jericho.*
>
> *Up to the walls of Jericho, he marched with spear in hand.*
> *"Go blow them ram horns," Joshua cried, "Cause the battle am in my hand."*
> *Then the lamb ram sheep horns began to blow, trumpets*

*began to sound,*
*Joshua commanded the children to shout, and the walls*
*   come tumbling down.*

*That morning,*
*Joshua fit the battle of Jericho, Jericho, Jericho;*
*Joshua fit the battle of Jericho, and the walls come tumbling*
*   down.*[6]

**Thea:** Whenever I used this song in one of my classes, I would have everybody get up, form a circle and start to sing this very, very slowly. Your foot will naturally make the right emphasis on the strong beat, and the stepping around the circle adds power to the words. Because you are doing exactly what the Israelites did in the scriptural account, and you are following the guidance built into the song itself. Now it is not hard for me to imagine how useful this song must have been to anybody who felt small, defenseless and up against some mighty formidable opposition. Like the old preacher would say, "I can see this, Church, with my spiritual eyesight," how the Israelites with next to nothing stood staring like crazy folks at the great, walled city of Jericho. And I can see them folks of Jericho looking down from the top of those wide, strong, unassailable walls, just a-pointing and a-laughing at that little old band Joshua had just led through the Jordan River. What a sight that is, to my soul.

Just when the Israelites are feeling lower than a wagon rut in the road, God tells them, through Joshua, that they are going to have to dig deep within the creativity of their souls if they are going to prevail against the assembled might—and ridicule—of the people of Jericho. There was going to be no army riding over the hill, no fiery bolts from heaven, no band of angels swooping down to their defense. No. There would be nothing but a song, and a step, and more determination than had ever been called up by anybody, anywhere, ever before.

**Bede:** The way you are laying it out before us makes me see just how important this song could be to our ancestors—and to anybody standing in the middle of the road with nothing but "a spear in hand," looking at a mighty big enemy looming up in the horizon. No matter who or what that enemy might be.

**Thea:** My appreciation for the deep spiritual insights of the folks who made up this song, and deemed it worthy to become a part of our inheritance, can be focused on one line: "Joshua commanded the children to shout, and the walls come tumbling down." Just feel the conviction in the song, just there. If you can get everybody in the church, in the community, in the circle, in the house to put their efforts into a common endeavor, if you can get them to join their voices into harmony and not be caught up in bickering, strife and discord, if you can get them to be patient in the face of anxiety-ridden adversity, if you can get them to hold on, and hold on and hold on to their energy and their nervous anticipation, and then to release it all in one tremendous shout!—well, then, you could easily mistake yourself for a group of Bible heroes, don't you think?

**Bede:** Amen. Yes. Amen.

**Thea:** I can also understand how just one person could call up all of that power, days after last singing in a ring-shout out in the woods some night. I can imagine some frightened woman being told that she was about to be whipped, or that her husband was about to be maimed, or that her children were about to be sold. I can imagine her being washed over in an ocean wave of panic. I can see her rushing from one place to another, seeking some solution to the threat looming ahead on her life-way. I can see her maybe deciding to grab her children and make a run for freedom. I can see even more panic set in. "How can I make it? How can I provide safety? And food? How can I 'make a way out of no way'?" And I can see her letting go of that choked-up anxiety as she starts humming this song—or some other song, just as strongly imprinted on her soul—and how she remembers the power of the ring-shout, and the closeness of her fellow singers. I can see her walking around the house, just a-singing and a-humming—sometimes even laughing and shouting—as she steals a blanket, or some food, or a knife, or even a gun. Maybe some money. Maybe a piece of paper, so that she can get somebody to forge a pass for her and for her children. I can see her finding the courage of her Bible family inside herself. And I can see her step off, down the road to the Jericho that stands before her.

**Bede:** O, Good Lord, yes.

**Thea:** And on that road, when the children start to whimper and panic for that "every once in a while," when no amount of cajoling could keep them quiet, I can hear her starting to sing this song, ever so quietly if she thought she was in danger of being overtaken, or a little more lively if she just wanted to divert the worry on their hearts. And I can hear her teaching this song to her children, and they just naturally fall into the spell of the song.

**Bede:** Because you cannot be afraid while you sing that song. The song just won't let you.

**Thea:** And that is the miracle of black sacred song. Like another song says, "I'm singing with a sword in my hand." If you hear that song, from the outside of the experience, as it were, then you might mistakenly think that the singer didn't have a care in the world. But from the inside of the experience, you would understand quite well that the song is being sung because there is a world of care in the singer's heart. The point is, even the walls of Jericho can come tumbling down, if you step to the song God gives you and don't bolt off foolishly, breaking your head on the mountainous walls confronting you. Here, Bede, put your hand in mine, and let's sing it, together:

> That morning,
> Joshua fit the battle of Jericho, Jericho, Jericho;
> Joshua fit the battle of Jericho, and the walls come tumbling
>     down.

**Bede:** You know, Thea, the whole time we've been talking about how the composers/singers put on "wings of faith" and became caught up in mystical transport, I have been thinking about another song that I think might fit your description of a ring-shout. I have always loved it, and have never been a part of singing it when people did not seem to have a spell of peace come over them. In fact, the song has been a sort of background theme to everything we have talked about so far. "We are climbing Jacob's ladder."

**Thea:** From the minute we mentioned that we came from some flying ancestors, we've been talking about one of the great unpreached realities of black spirituality. Now, it really is the true truth that we are a people mighty devoted to dreams and visions. Ain't nothing Freudian about us. The only dreams that give us fits are the ones we can't squeeze a prophecy out of.

**Bede:** Jacob's dream isn't sung about very much in most Christian churches. And I don't remember very many sermons preached about him when I was growing up. But our folks sure did love to sing about that ladder. And the song could go on and on, for almost as long as it took to get up that ladder.

**Thea:** That's why it is wise for you to claim it as a ring-shout.

**Bede:** And the most interesting thing about the song is that Jacob is always being talked to, exhorted, or is otherwise the object of the song. The singers do not use their "wings of faith" to become *Jacob*.

**Thea:** And that surely is not due to humility. After all, they get possessed enough in the prophetic call to become God the Almighty when they sing, "Go down, Moses."

**Bede:** No, it wasn't humility. That might be what you called the unpreached reality. Our ancestor singers kept on identifying with the angelic messengers—or "God's heavenly stand-ins"—in these songs. "*We* are climbing Jacob's ladder," is what the song says. And they shout, "wake up, Jacob." And in the first one collected, "Wrestle on, Jacob," they really get into the spirit of the story.

> *I hold my brother [sister, all the members, etc.] with a*
>   *trembling hand,*
> *The Lord will bless my soul.*
> *Wrestle on, Jacob, Jacob, day is a-breaking,*
> *Wrestle on, Jacob, Oh, Lord, I would not let him go.*[7]

To realize that they are singing as if they are the very

angels of God is to turn upside down many notions of servanthood, discipleship and prophecy that seem to reinforce a sense of inferiority and doubt. These folks put themselves into holy trances, sang the holy stories of faith and whipped themselves into believing that they were the Bible heroes once again on the earth to serve the people.

**Thea:** Like I said, the singer lifts the Church, the people, to a higher level of understanding, feeling, motivation and participation.

**Bede:** Well, you can't get to a much higher level than one of the angels of God. What is important to me is the prophetic task being assumed. The singers are saying, once we get into our trance and are lifted up to heaven, that just like St. John on the island of Patmos was taken up to see the vision of the last day, then we, too, have messages we must bring back to earth for the good of the members. No vision is a private vision. The preachers knew that.

**Thea:** And still know it. When a good preacher shifts into the last part of the sermon, everybody within hearing gets ready to step off onto the streets paved with gold and see all the sights of the heavenly city, Jerusalem.

**Bede:** So, the way I understand it is this. When we get ourselves into a vision-place, when we use the songs to see some truth of God more closely than the world will allow us to glimpse, we cannot come back to earth and take up our ordinary daily-ness. No, we have to run through the streets and tell the good news: "I heard from heaven today. Bless God, and bless you, too, I heard from heaven today."

**Thea:** "Oh, children, you ought to been there, a-setting in the kingdom, to hear sweet Jordan roll."

**Bede:** And when the singer says, "meet me, Jesus, meet me/ meet me in the middle of the air. And if these wings don't fit me, I'll try me another pair," then we have to know that the song must be taken very seriously. We need those wings to do the work of God. Our very prayer, our mystical union, is for the good of the community.

**Thea:** That's absolutely right. *We* are climbing Jacob's ladder. And only the angels of God were permitted passage on those rungs. Scripture tells us that "the angels were ascending and descending it," and that Jacob woke up from his dream and called it "the gate of heaven" (Genesis 28:10 ff.).

> *We are climbing Jacob's ladder, We are climbing Jacob's ladder,*
> *We are climbing Jacob's ladder, Soldiers of the cross.*
> *Every rung goes higher and higher...*
>
> *If you love Him, why not serve Him...*
> *Rise and shine, and give God glory....*[8]

**Bede:** Without a vision the people perish, we are told. And if we can be lifted up, for the service of the people, to receive a message for the good of all, why, then, I guess we ought to try on some wings. Amen.

**Thea:** Amen.

## For Reflection

- *Recall times in your life when you felt called to deepen your*

response to the Word of God, either through singing, giving
witness or speaking up in some other way. Did you respond
to those urges? Why or why not? How did you feel when
you made your decision?

- Listen to some of the music discussed in this meditation. In
  what ways might you incorporate these songs into your
  daily prayer and meditation?

- Take a few moments and remember some of the people in
  your life who have been powerful guides in your spiritual
  development. Speak with them in prayer, thanking them for
  their guidance and support.

- In what ways would you ask the help of the Holy Spirit to
  gain "wings of faith"? How do you hope those wings will
  enable you to contribute to the good of the faith
  community?

## Closing Prayer

Send forth your Holy Spirit, O God, you who love us
and care for us with a mother's love and a father's care.
Support us with your power and grace, especially when
we attempt to lift ourselves up from the chaos and
distractions that surround us. Give us the Gift of Wisdom,
O God, that we might see you in all things, hear you
speaking to us in song, word and silence. Because we
believe that we are truly an Alleluia! people, teach us to
sing your praises, and tell the world how we made it over.
Amen.

## Closing Song

*We are climbing Jacob's ladder, We are climbing*
*    Jacob's ladder,*
*We are climbing Jacob's ladder, Soldiers of the cross.*
*Every round goes higher, and higher...*

*Rise and shine, and give God glory...*

## Notes

[1] *Say Amen, Somebody*, a film by George T. Nierenberg, Pacific Arts Video Records, PAVR-547, 1984.

[2] "The Gift of African American Sacred Song," *Lead Me, Guide Me*, n. p.

[3] Found in *The Collected Works of St. Teresa of Avila, Volume I*, trans. Kieran Kavanaugh, O.C.D., and Otilo Rodriguez, O.C.D. (Washington, D.C.: Institute of Carmelite Studies, 1987), p. 173.

[4] Found in *John of the Cross: Selected Writings*, ed., intro. Kieran Kavanaugh, O.C.D. (New York: Paulist Press, 1987), p. 294.

[5] Du Bois, *The Souls of Black Folk*, p. 211.

[6] This complete text can be found in *The Books of American Negro Spirituals*, 2 vols. (New York: Da Capo Press, 1969), in Volume I, p. 57.

[7] Allen, et al., *Slave Songs of the United States*, #6.

[8] *Lead Me, Guide Me*, #54.

# DAY FOUR
## Standing at the Crossroads

### Coming Together in the Spirit

Then Jesus told them a parable about their need to pray always and not to lose heart. He said, "In a certain city there was a judge who neither feared God nor had respect for people. In that city there was a widow who kept coming to him and saying, 'Grant me justice against my opponent.' For a while he refused; but later he said to himself, 'Though I have no fear of God and no respect for anyone, yet because this widow keeps bothering me, I will grant her justice so that she may not wear me out by continually coming.' And the Lord said, "Listen to what the unjust judge says. And will not God grant justice to his chosen ones who cry to him day and night? Will he delay long in helping them? I tell you, he will quickly grant justice to them. And yet when the Son of man comes, will he find faith on earth?" (Luke 18:1-8)

### Defining Our Thematic Context

Interwoven throughout this retreat has been the theme of confrontational prayer. One of the marks of African American spirituality that identifies it with biblical spirituality is the ease with which the composers/singers/ performers "knock on heaven's door," demanding God's attention. For our purposes confrontational prayer must be considered under a double scrutiny. First, the believers (in the tradition of Job, Jeremiah, Ezekiel, Jonah and Mary) question the designs of God directly and with little hesitation, expecting to be answered. Second, the songs and prayers of the African American tradition challenge the individual and the participating community to stand up and be accounted for. In the songs, prayers and anecdotes of faith, all involved are at the crossroads, often called "the cross" in this tradition. The two symbols were not originally the same, with the crossroads being the starting place of all western African religious rituals. With the cross of Jesus Christ introduced to their set of symbols, the transplanted Africans were able to layer one symbol upon the other and double the meaning. Thus they opened up their understanding of righteous behavior to include both Creator and created servant. As we have already discovered in our Afri-centered prayer, multiple meanings open to us in the singing of the songs. No contradictions are allowed to exist when we are transformed and lifted up by song.

## Opening Song

*Down at the cross where my Savior died,*
*Down where for cleansing from sin I cried,*
*There to my heart was the blood applied;*
*Glory to His name.*

*Glory to His name, Glory to His name!*
*There to my heart was the blood applied;*
*Glory to His name.*

*I am so wondrously saved from sin,*
*Jesus so sweetly abides within;*
*There at the cross where He took me in;*
*Glory to His name.*

*Glory to His name, Glory to His name!*
*There to my heart was the blood applied;*
*Glory to His name.*[1]

## Opening Prayer

Oh, dear God who lives and reigns above, I call upon you to please "lay your head in the window," and incline your care toward me today. I am kneeling in the wilderness of the world, seeking your protection and your help. Even though storms rage in my life and waves of danger assail me, I am sure and certain that your presence will say to all the troubles of my life, "Peace, be still." At the time of his greatest suffering, when your beloved son, Jesus, cried out to you, you heard him and restored him to life. At the crossroads of my life, O God, I ask for all your mercy, all your love, all your grace. Help me to walk steadfast in your ways. Amen.

# RETREAT SESSION FOUR

**Bede:** We may see ourselves as a "chosen race, a royal priesthood, a holy nation, God's own people," but it is a mighty hard struggle to keep that vision in our minds and to act out that description. Especially when the storms of life are raging....

**Thea:** Which is why the rest of the song says, "Stand by me."

**Bede:** We have sung and prayed about how the old folks found a new God in this new wilderness called *enslavement,* and how they called "Come by here" to God, and how God heard the cry of the oppressed. I see that encounter to be a confrontation.

**Thea:** How so? God did not confront the people. At least, not in the way recorded in the Bible, when the children of Israel would harden their hearts, turn deaf ears to the prophets and find themselves in exile and enslavement because they had begun to choose death over life, in spite of what they told Moses.

**Bede:** No, the encounter-turned-into-confrontation was much more complicated than that. And I think that what happened becomes one of the central foundations of our black faith. You cannot sing the songs, or be immersed in the faith of the African American Christians we are walking with here, and not see that the problem of evil, of sin in the world, is just as much a problem for black people as it is for any theologian anywhere in the world at any time. We talked about this before: Our African American ancestors of faith and blood knew that they were not guilty of some originating sin, and therefore had not earned what the Bible called punishment for sin. No matter how hard the argument was pushed, not even when some of the theologians defending slavery said that Africans had been born marked with the mark of Cain—

**Thea:** With black skin, you mean—

**Bede:** Yes, marked with black skin, which—they said—

was the color of sin, the color of darkness, the color of evil. With all of that being told to them, the geniuses of our faith inheritance were strong in their conviction that they, too, had shoes—and wings, and robes, and harps and crowns—and they were going to walk all over God's heaven, just as surely as would their oppressors and owners.

**Thea:** Maybe more surely, since they had such fun singing, "Everybody talking 'bout heaven ain't going there."

**Bede:** But, like we talked about before, this song was an act of faith. All the singing about heaven that they did, and that we do, cannot banish the hell of the here and now for more than a few minutes. Just long enough to catch our holy breath, as it were. "Oh, give me a little time to pray," the singer pleads.

**Thea:** That's true, my brother. And you and I know this as well as anybody can. Standing at the crossroads, or standing down at the cross, it's the same place, and the same decision needs to be made. Will you fall to the snares of the devil, or will you continue to "wait on the Lord"? Not all the black sacred songs are happy, shouting songs. No, indeed. Dr. Du Bois was right when he called them the sorrow songs. And Frederick Douglass told us to be careful even with the songs that seemed happy—that there was an undertow of sadness and sorrow that could pull a person into a whirlpool of despair if they weren't careful. Douglass spoke as only one who was "on the inside looking out" could speak, when he said:

> I have often been utterly astonished, since I came to the North, to find persons who could speak of the singing, among slaves, as evidence of their contentment and happiness. It is impossible to

conceive of a greater mistake. Slaves sing most when they are most unhappy. The songs of the slave represent the sorrows of his heart; and he is relieved by them, only as an aching heart is relieved by its tears. At least, such is my experience. I have often sung to drown my sorrow, but seldom to express my happiness. Crying for joy, and singing for joy, were alike uncommon to me while in the jaws of slavery. The singing of a man cast away upon a desolate island might be as appropriately considered as evidence of contentment and happiness, as the singing of a slave; the songs of the one and of the other are prompted by the same emotion.[2]

**Bede:** Every mother's child who has had to carry the wounds of oppression, sorrow and the aftermath of sin knows what Douglass is talking about. The songs of our people, Thea, are tears that flow upward, to heaven, calling on the Son of God, it seems, to "lay his head in the window" and show mercy to his people.

There are some songs that break my heart to hear them sung, because they take me to the axis point of black faith—to the cross. "My Lord, what a mourning," the song says. And that ain't no misprint, Bede. "What a mourning, when the stars refused to shine." Or "Were you there, when they crucified my Lord?" Amen. Where were you standing, believer, unbeliever, when the sweetest man who ever walked the earth was hung up on a cross, as a sign and a question mark to the world? Where do *you* stand when goodness itself is crucified?

**Bede:** That same feeling comes through when the singer tells us, "I wish I had a-died in Egypt land." The anguish of telling the true truth, as you always call it, Thea, means that the valley of the shadow of death has to be described in terms just as clear as those used to describe the contours of heaven. Except that you don't need a mystical vision to see the valley.

**Thea:**

> Oh, I went to the rock to hide my face,
> The rock cried out, "No hiding place!"
> There's no hiding place down there.
>
> Oh, the rock cried, "I'm burning too,"
> Oh, the rock cried, "I'm burning too,"
> Oh, the rock cried, "I'm burning too,
> I want to go to heaven as well as you."
> There's no hiding place down there.[3]

**Bede:** You got to choose the path on which you will tread. No one can walk it for you, you've got to walk it by yourself.

**Thea:** There's a song of sorrow that not a lot of people seem to know. I think it captures the utter anguish that is the ground of all the faith we have been talking about since this retreat began. Kathleen Battle sings it beautifully, in the concert she did with Jessye Norman at Carnegie Hall:

> Lord, how come me here; Lord, how come me here; Lord,
>     how come me here?
> I wish I never was born....
> They ain't no freedom here, Lord; they ain't no
> freedom here; they ain't no freedom here—
> I wish I never was born....
> They treat me so mean here, Lord; they treat me so
> mean; they treat me so mean—
> I wish I never was born....
> They sold my children away, Lord; they sold my

*children away; they sold my children away—*
*I wish I never was born....*[4]

**Bede:** Oh, bless God. Bless God. "I wish I never was born." I wonder if some of our retreatants haven't felt that way at some time in their lives. That is just what I mean when I say that our spirituality is confrontational. That song is a direct commentary on the laments of Job. No, even more, it is a lamentation and can be uttered only by someone who is as close to God as one can get. Like Job and Jeremiah, the Africans who became believers came to God with the "smell of life on them." And they confronted God—

**Thea:** And they encountered the answer to their lament even as they confronted the Almighty. They experienced the presence of God in the midst of their suffering, death and destruction. No matter how deep the despair, they were talking and singing and praying and weeping to a God who understood. After all, that is the meaning of the crossroads and the cross. The devil stands at the juncture, telling us all about our trials and tribulations, just like he did when he found Jesus in the desert. "You're hungry and tired, and confused," says the tempter. "You're filled with doubts and you are feeling alienated, divorced from hope, and lost. Why look to the heavens for an answer? Here is bread, and comfort and prestige. Here are my ministering hands, my immediate comforts. Curse God, and come with me." Oh, we have all heard the whisperings of the devil as we stand at the junction in the road, wondering which way to turn.

**Bede:** Many a believing daughter and son of God has cried out, with Jesus: "My God, my God! Why have you forsaken me?" Many a child of God has looked at the cross that looms at the crossroads, and said: I cannot bear the weight.

**Thea:** Bede, after all these years, in my own heart of hearts, I no longer ask why so many of our sisters and brothers seem to give up hope. I can only marvel that so many seem to hold on to the anchor of faith in the face of the buffeting storms.

**Bede:** Amen. We look to the mountains, whence cometh our help. And we cry for our deliverance.

**Thea:** And in the cry, we are delivered. The whole point is to see that we can fall down in the dirt and "curse God, and die." We can choose that path and none can gainsay our choice. When we lose our strength to carry the cross, we can lay down the burden and let the world cover us. Or we can look at the cross and see the way out.

**Bede:** If you look at the cross, you see the answer. Jesus was at the crossroads every blessed day of his earthly life. Right up to the end, hanging there, he could have said, "No. I refuse to love these people, or you, anymore." And that would have been the end of it; the end of it all. "Why have you forsaken me?" is not the last thing Jesus said from the cross.

**Thea:** He said, "Father, into your hands I commend my spirit" (Luke 23:46).

**Bede:** The songs are tears to relieve the anguish. If we are to respect the original composers and singers of these great songs, we must come back to their understanding, over and over. Yes, they knew the salty tears of exile, oppression, death and destruction. Yes, they knew the crushing weight of rape, abuse, disfigurement and disease. They considered it all, turning over in their hearts all these woundings-unto-death. And they declared to their turbulent and sorrowful hearts—and to the world that may have been listening to their calls: Because we know the resurrection, we can remain steadfast as we are being crucified.

**Thea:** And that is where the mystical prayer that they learned in the crucible of faith became a means of salvation once again. They stood at the cross and saw *themselves*, hanging in the middle of the air. They saw a Jesus who knew every tear and every heartbreak. They knew that even the Son of God knew what it meant to live and die a godforsaken existence. But they were believers of a kind not seen since the days of the Bible. Because they sang themselves into the tomb, and out again.

> *I've been 'buked and I've been scorned, I've been 'buked and*
> *I've been scorned, children.*
> *I've been 'buked and I've been scorned, I've been talked*
> *about sho's you born.*
>
> *There is trouble all over this world, there is trouble all over*
> *this world, children.*
> *There is trouble all over this world, there is trouble all over*
> *this world.*
>
> *Ain't gwine lay my 'ligion down, Aint gwine lay my 'ligion*
> *down, children.*
> *Ain't gwine lay my 'ligion down, Ain't gwine lay my*
> *'ligion down.*
>
> *Gonna tell my Lordy when I get home, Gonna tell my*
> *Lordy when I get home, children.*
> *Gonna tell my Lordy when I get home, Just how long they*
> *been treating me wrong.*[5]

**Bede:** There is no other answer to the destruction of sin. "Ain't no grave can hold my body down." There are a million graves and a million deaths waiting for every one. And none will be any more permanent than the one that was a way-station for our sweet Savior. The Book of Deuteronomy brings us the story of the great decision at the crossroads, and any of our ancestors who heard the story of the Jews at the edge of the desert would have been able to see themselves in the same setting with the same challenge placed before them.

> You know how we lived in the land of Egypt, and how we came through the midst of the nations through which you passed. You have seen their detestable things, the filthy idols of wood and stone, of silver and gold, that were among them. It may be that there is among you a man or woman or a family or tribe, whose heart is already turning away from the LORD our God to serve the gods of those nations. It may be that there is among you a root sprouting poisonous and bitter growth. All who hear the words of this oath and bless themselves, thinking in their hearts, "We are safe, even though we go our own stubborn ways" (thus bringing disaster on moist and dry alike)....
>
> Surely, for this commandment that I am commanding you today is not too hard for you, nor is it too far away. It is not in heaven, that you should say, "Who will go up to heaven for us and get it for us, so that we may hear it and observe it?" Neither is it beyond the sea, that you should say, "Who will cross to the other side of the sea for us, and get it for us so that we may hear it and observe it?" No, the word is very near to you; it is in your mouth and in your heart for you to observe.
>
> See, I have set before you today life and prosperity, death and adversity.... I call heaven and

> earth to witness against you today that I have set
> before you life and death, blessings and curses.
> Choose life so that you and your descendants may
> live, loving the LORD your God, obeying him, and
> holding fast.... (Deuteronomy 29:16-19; 30:1-15,
> 19-20)

Yes, Thea, the word was very near them, in their hearts and in their mouths. They did "go up to heaven" though, to get the "title to their freedom" from God. And we, their descendants, are still cleaving to God.

**Thea:** It ought to be clear to anybody who can hear the song being sung, "Up above my head, I hear music in the air, I know there must be a heaven somewhere." It ought to be clear that, having been rebuked and scorned a thousand ways to Sunday, these believing people performed a mighty miracle when they snatched life out of the jaws of death. Standing steadfast, Bede, standing steadfast—that's the key to the crossroads, and to the cross. They confronted the cross, and let the cross answer them. They remained where they stood. Unlike most of the disciples, they did not turn and run from the sight of the Savior on the cross. They had been there, they had seen many a mother's child "whipped up Calvary's hill." Even in the face of the unimaginable grief, seeing God hanging from a tree, they could still soothe his dying breath with a song of understanding.

**Bede:** Please, Thea, sing it for us one more time.

**Thea:**

> *They crucified my Lord, And He never said a mumbaling
> word,*

*They crucified my Lord, And He never said a mumbaling word,*
*Not a word, not a word, not a word.*

*They whipped Him up Calvary's hill, And He never said a mumbaling word,*
*They whipped Him up Calvary's hill, And He never said a mumbaling word,*
*Not a word, not a word, not a word.*

*They nailed Him to the tree, And He never said a mumbaling word,*
*They nailed Him to the tree, And He never said a mumbaling word,*
*Not a word, not a word, not a word.*

*They pierced Him in the side, And He never said a mumbaling word,*
*They pierced Him in the side, And He never said a mumbaling word,*
*Not a word, not a word, not a word.*

*The blood came streaming down, And He never said a mumbaling word,*
*The blood came streaming down, And He never said a mumbaling word,*
*Not a word, not a word, not a word.*

*He hung His head and died, And He never said a mumbaling word,*
*He hung His head and died, And He never said a mumbaling word,*
*Not a word, not a word, not a word.*[6]

**Bede:** Let all that is within me cry "Holy." When we stand at the crossroads in the need of prayer, we deliver ourselves into the hand of God. And we are delivered.

**Thea:** And we are delivered. Amen. Amen. Amen.

## For Reflection

- *Visualize yourself at the scene of the crucifixion. Imagine yourself standing next to Mary, the Mother of Jesus. From the cross Jesus looks at you and speaks to you. What does he say? How do you respond to him?*

- *What griefs and heartbreaks would you lay at the foot of the cross, asking that you be healed through the suffering of Christ?*

- *What crossroads are you facing in your life today? In what ways would you say to Jesus, "Stand by me"?*

- *Remember one or two occasions when you doubted which path to take at some juncture in your life. Reflect on how God was present. Remember the gratitude you felt.*

- *In what ways can you can share your sense of gratitude with others? With members of your family? Friends? Through volunteer work? Through the support of group prayer?*

## Closing Prayer

Oh, God, we stand in the need of deliverance, of mercy.

Oh, God, we stand at the crossroads of our lives today, asking that the power of your grace fill us and make us steadfast in our determination to walk in your ways. Guided as we are by the lives and example of our sister, Thea, and our brother, Bede, may we hunger and thirst only for justice and righteousness. May we be filled with your Holy Spirit, so that our light may shine in the darkness that sometimes threatens our days.

Give us a discerning heart and a mind filled with your wisdom, that we might hear your voice calling to us in those times when we seem to stumble or stray from the path.

Through the prayers and help of Thea and Bede, teach us to be unafraid.

Amen.

## Closing Song

Down at the cross where my Savior died,
Down where for cleansing from sin I cried,
There to my heart was the blood applied;
Glory to His name.

Glory to His name, Glory to His name!
There to my heart was the blood applied;
Glory to His name.

I am so wondrously saved from sin,
Jesus so sweetly abides within;
There at the cross where He took me in;
Glory to His name.

## Notes

[1] *Lead Me, Guide Me,* #46.
[2] Frederick Douglass, "Narrative of the Life of Frederick Douglass," found in *The Classic Slave Narratives,* ed. Henry Louis Gates, Jr. (New York: Mentor Books, 1987), p. 263.
[3] *Songs of Zion,* #141.
[4] Kathleen Battle and Jessye Norman. *Spirituals in Concert.* Deutsche

Grammophon. 1991. CD 429-790-2.

[5] *Lead Me, Guide Me*, #53.

[6] *Songs of Zion*, #101.

# DAY FIVE

## *Walking and Talking With Jesus*

### *Coming Together in the Spirit*

> So Jacob rose early in the morning, and he took the
> stone that he had put under his head and set it up
> for a pillar and poured oil on the top of it. He called
> that place Bethel ["the house of God"]... Then Jacob
> made a vow, saying, "If God will be with me, and
> will keep me in this way that I go, and will give me
> bread to eat and clothing to wear, so that I come
> again to my father's house in peace, then the LORD
> shall be my God, and this stone, which I have set up
> for a pillar, shall be God's house; and of all that you
> give me I surely give one tenth to you."
> (Genesis 28:18-22)

As role models for us, Jacob and his beloved, Rachel, have
some surprising habits and characteristics, ways of
responding to the Divine that might give us pause, forcing
us to reflect on the meaning of covenant in our lives. The
covenant at Bethel occurs on the morning after Jacob's
dream about the angels traversing the ladder between
heaven and earth. During this encounter at the crossroads,
God establishes the divine side of the covenant. Since
Jacob is the grandson of Abraham and Sarah, and the son
of Isaac and Rebecca, one would think that Jacob had no
reason to qualify his response to God's initiating promises.

After all, God's promises had come true for his relatives—why should Jacob doubt the power of God? But he does qualify his response. His side of the bargain is dotted with "ifs," to the point that any complete acceptance of God in Jacob's life will be many years in the future. In effect, Jacob puts God on probation, demanding material signs and wonders before he will declare himself for God.

Twenty-one years into his sojourn among "the people of the east," after marrying both Leah and Rachel, the daughters of his uncle, Laban, and after also propagating children with Bilhah and Zilpah, two enslaved women, Jacob had grown more or less comfortable with his arrangement. After all, no matter how manipulative Laban might have been in undermining his contractual agreements with Jacob, Jacob was quite proficient in regaining advantage of the situation. He had a history of actualizing the blessing bestowed upon him at birth by any means necessary. Perhaps surprisingly, no matter how selfish Jacob might have been in demanding collateral from God, God was faithful in providing the substance of all Jacob's demands. However, when the women in this arrangement had grown tired of living under Laban's domination, they joined themselves into a strategy by which they—and all that Jacob claimed as his own—would be removed from the control of Laban. When Jacob agreed that it was, indeed, possible for him to return to Isaac's house in peace, the household organized itself in the grandest tradition of the biblical patriarchs and Jacob removed them all westward.

Immediately before this departure from the house of Laban, Rachel acts both to improve their chances of successful relocation and to severely limit her father's power over his descendants. "...Laban had gone to shear his sheep, and Rachel stole her father's household gods" (Genesis 31:19). The statues and other artifacts that were the sacred household objects were as symbolic as the stone at Bethel, anointed by Jacob as a sign of his bonding with God. In stealing these symbols of divine favor, Rachel both collapsed her father's sense of security and bolstered her own. There are few acts of appropriation more daring, more radical or more unexpected—in the Bible or elsewhere in literature. Rachel and her sister, Leah, by pushing Jacob to make his return to his father's house, mirrored the act of Rebecca when she urged Jacob to steal his brother's inheritance (the patriarchal blessing of the first-born male) and then to place himself in exile among his relatives "in the east." Jacob and his wives demonstrated a capacity for seizing every advantage and every opportunity, for their survival and for their development as a family, as the prophesied "nation without number."

## *Defining Our Thematic Context*

Continuing our meditation on the crossroads of faith, we are asked, this day, to consider our responses to the redemptive act of Jesus on the cross. By meditating upon the choices presented, "to choose either life or death, blessing or curse" (as Moses articulates it in the Book of Deuteronomy), we will be guided by the songs and lessons of African American spirituality to see that not only must all believers know themselves as a chosen people, but we must accept the responsibility inherent in being a choosing people, as well.

## *Opening Song*

*God sent his Son, they called him Jesus;*

*He came to love, heal, and forgive;*
*He lived and died to buy my pardon,*
*An empty grave is there to prove my Savior lives.*

*Because He lives I can face tomorrow;*
*Because He lives all fear is gone;*
*Because I know He holds the future,*
*And life is worth the living just because He lives.*

*How sweet to hold a newborn baby,*
*And feel the pride, and joy He gives;*
*But greater still the calm assurance,*
*This child can face uncertain days because He lives.*

*Because He lives I can face tomorrow;*
*Because He lives all fear is gone;*
*Because I know He holds the future,*
*And life is worth the living, just because He lives.*

*And then one day I'll cross the river;*
*I'll fight life's final war with pain;*
*And then as death gives way to vict'ry,*
*I'll see the lights of glory and I'll know He lives.*

*Because He lives I can face tomorrow;*
*Because He lives all fear is gone;*
*Because I know He holds the future,*
*And life is worth the living just because He lives.*[1]

## RETREAT SESSION FIVE

**Thea:** I do love that old song. I can remember many an old lady in our neighborhood and in our church singing that song whenever they just got filled up with the goodness of

God. No matter where I went, no matter what church affiliation I might claim, that song touches something in my heart.

**Bede:** Well, Thea, it just proves something we know about black folks, and our culture. If it works, pick it up and use it.

**Thea:** Bede, you know as well as I do that that is not a tendency restricted to black people. Especially in matters of religion. There's many a shouting Baptist and a get-happy Pentecostal churchgoer who owes her ecstatic style to some Africans who were singing and praising their God outside the tent during some of those old-time camp meetings a hundred years ago. They wouldn't let us inside the tent, so we had church where we were. And before you knew it, our church changed their church.

**Bede:** That should be the core of all our religious experience. If it is compelling, it is also attractive. People followed the sound of the singing, and many a tent got emptied before the meeting was over. We cannot have culture, or church, or art, or family, without an awful lot of give and take.

**Thea:** That's right. That's why so many of the songs we sing in the black church have been gathered from every place we have ever been. We made "Amazing Grace" shake off the sounds of Scottish bagpipes, and put on some African dissonance when we took up with it. Isaac Watts and Fanny Crosby and the Wesleys composed some glorious hymns and anthems, and we have "put our mouths on them," as Zora Hurston would say.[2]

**Bede:** And black singing saints made room in their hearts and throats for all of them. If the message is true, and the grace is there, then open up your self and let the song sound forth.

**Thea:** That's some real preaching, Bede. And the true truth. Black folks respect good theology and good art. We expect one to contain the other, I think.

**Bede:** "Because He Lives" is a favorite hymn of mine, too. I dwell on the part that says, "I can face tomorrow... Because I know he holds the future." The future was something the earliest enslaved Africans had to learn about, if they were to survive. They understood the past very well, because that was the time in which the ancestors lived. And they understood the present, and saw it extending out to the very edge of their understanding. The present was when you stood in the middle of the circle of life, on the axis point, and made your ethical/social decisions, keeping in mind both the instruction of the ancestors and the needs of the children. You held the past and the foreseeable future in your hands.

**Thea:** Slavery sure took the ground from under their feet, separating them from their past, bringing chaos into the present and making every tomorrow a cause for anxiety and fear. It took tremendous faith to even want to see a tomorrow, let alone trust its control to the hand of anyone, much less a God they were just learning about. Oh, but what they learned....

> *What manner of man is this, Who died upon the tree?*
> *What manner of man is this, Who set the captives free?*
> *Oh, you know, He walked upon the water, and He calmed*
>     *the raging sea;*

*What manner of man is this, Who gave His life for you and me?*[3]

That's a song that just makes you want to get up and make a ring-shout, isn't it? The theology in this song, and the way the great singers like Mahalia Jackson or Brother Joe May can belt it out, tells you volumes about the way our ancestors found Jesus at the crossroads and decided to make a covenant with him. He brought them joy, joy, joy in their souls.

**Bede:** And he performed acts of righteousness. The suffering servant, the triumphant king, the word-delivering prophet, the resurrected Savior—all these Christological themes get sung about. And just this little part of this one song does a pretty good job of locating the themes most important to the old ones. He performed mighty miracles. He hung on the tree. He gave his life for me. Jesus did what God required, no matter the personal cost. Jesus was a flesh and blood "child of God"—

**Thea:** Whose mama rocked him in a weary land—

**Bede:** Who told people what he was going to do, and then did it. Righteousness.

**Thea:** When we look at the images in "What Manner of Man Is This," we see enduring themes that folks never get tired of preaching and singing about. First, Jesus died upon *the* tree. That is his crossroads. It is also that mystical place the singers favor so much. Jesus is caught between heaven and earth, between his earthly past and his heavenly future, between heaven and hell, between the blessing and the curse, between life and death. They knew the importance of where he hung. Now see where the song takes us immediately, Bede? "He set the captives free." The song takes us from the beginning of his ministry, when he stood up in the synagogue and told the world what he was about, full circle to the ending when Jesus "did just what he said." Yes, Bede, your theme of righteousness is sounding strong, right here and now. I like to think that the image of Jesus walking on water, and his calming the raging sea, had to have a special resonance for a people whose greatest trauma was incited by the raging sea of the middle passage.

**Bede:** Those two images are linked in hundreds of songs. Walking on the water, calming the raging sea, uttering "Peace; be still"—those sometimes seem to be the major work of Jesus in the Spirituals and the gospel songs.

**Thea:** The sight of Jesus suspended forever "way in the middle of the air," redefining the boundaries of human existence and experience, had a profound effect on our ancestors, Bede. Once they recognized the personal redemption offered to them, they ran out and named almost every church "Bethel." They had a vision of a promise from heaven, and they hooked their futures to that historical event. "Remember that day? Oh, I remember it well...He saved my soul from burning Hell," another song states. When Jesus turned life upside down, way back there on Golgotha, he did all he had to do for these folks. They didn't need to be convinced over a long period of probation—like Jacob. No. Their captivity was not symbolic, nor did it have internalized rewards. They needed a God of real power, and one who would hear their prayer quickly.

**Bede:** And also unlike Jacob in many respects, the singers of these songs (our grandmother and grandfather Doctors of the Church), did not hesitate to engage themselves in living up to their end of the covenant. Righteous behavior became their code.

**Thea:** You are absolutely right. The stories we call "slave narratives" are filled with examples of African American Christians shaming their owners, their so-called "masters" and "mistresses," with "Christian" behavior that would have humbled any of the canonized saints. In fact, it is a variation on this behavior that Harriet Beecher Stowe exploited in *Uncle Tom's Cabin*.

**Bede:** They had many witnesses asking the question, "What manner of woman, what manner of man, is this?" How could the cast-off and degraded, "the wretched of the earth," become such powerful witnesses of righteous Christian behavior that even unbelievers were humbled in the face of their actions? The question haunts many people, even today.

**Thea:** Jesus was the model and the standard of behavior, after all. These men and women of Africa came to America, most of them, fully formed in culture. They brought a spirituality, a sense of culture, a system of philosophical and theological reflection and highly developed skills of creativity. When they found that the circle of their lives had, indeed, been broken, they set about forging a new circle—with Jesus on the cross as the axis point. Their reliance on spirit-possession rituals allowed them to identify more easily with a whole new family of ancestors—the biblical heroes and the ecclesiastical communion of saints. Their immersion in oral-based culture and their dance-based creativity allowed them to disseminate their adapted and appropriated cultural insights to a wide audience, with an immediacy that is still unsurpassed. They had to find ways to calm the raging sea of their perpetual enslavement and permanent exile. And they still had to find ways to live lives that honored their ancestors (those of faith and family) and teach their children to live with integrity and purpose. So, they saw the best of men hanging on "the tree," and they decided to do what Jesus did: live a righteous life.

**Bede:** And call others to live the same righteous life. After all, the encounter with God has to go beyond the gaining of knowledge. The question arises, almost immediately: "What is your personal response? What are you going to do in the light of this revelation?"

**Thea:** So, they combed through the Scriptures and through their own trials and tribulations—

**Bede:** And they remembered old stories of old ways, from the homeland—

**Thea:** And they painted a portrait of a Jesus who could be a guiding light in the midst of the darkness that seemed to engulf them, everywhere.

**Bede:** When we think of how many West African societies were organized around a feeling of the wholeness of the circle, we can understand how important the virtue of generosity was to the Africans transplanted to the Americas. All of our talk about a crossroads experience implies a sense of generosity as the guiding factor in making decisions. No individual can be selfish, be individualistic, if you will, when making a decision in this worldview. Their thought went like this: "I am here. Which "way" shall I go? I cannot deviate from the path of my ancestors, or from the guidance and instruction of my elders. That would be to dishonor them and to call their spirits to haunt and torment me until I would go mad. Nor can I make such a path that would cut me off from my children and the children of my people. No. Unless I decide to make a way that will be safe for them to traverse, I will not be considered worthy to be honored as their elder and, someday, as their ancestor—whose memory will be kept alive in the praise songs of our people." A great many African folktales and epics are concerned with a central character who decides to go off alone and becomes entangled in a jungle of threats, disasters and anxieties.[4] Either by word, deed or intention, in these African philosophies the person who chooses to be *selfish*, subordinating the needs of the community to the individual's desires, chooses the path of isolation and death. The life and work of Jesus would have been seen as exemplary of these ideals, of this ethical tradition.

**Thea:** The songs tell of many other virtues linked to the generosity of Jesus. And these virtues become a textbook for healthy living and guides for establishing an effective therapy for combating the worst pain of the suffering and oppression of slavery and racism. The whole system was designed to break the spirit and to induce such severe depression that every man, woman and child who was touched by slavery's icy hand would feel the utter isolation and brokenness that fills the meaning of "sometimes I feel like a motherless child" and "I wish I'd never been born." The spirituality we are praying over here fills up Toni Morrison's great meditation on the breaking of the human spirit, her novel, *Beloved*. I know Morrison is sensitive to this notion because she takes the title of the novel from Paul's Letter to the Romans, in a reference that tells us how God brings the broken-spirited into a healing circle:

> *I will call them my people,*
> *which were not my people;*
> *and her beloved,*
> *which was not beloved.*[5]

**Bede:** So, to the principle of generosity, you have added the notion of communal identity as part of the picture of righteous behavior. And I would say that flowing from both are the virtues of compassion and forgiveness. The sacred songs are filled with stories of Jesus demonstrating both. I think that the song, "he never said a mumbaling word," captures both virtues. In the Passion narrative, we are told that Jesus told Pilate that nobody could do nothing to him that he, Jesus the Son of God, did not allow them to do (John 19:11). And Jesus could not unleash a display of divine power, and not have forgiveness in his heart, forgiveness based on the fact that he knew what was in the hearts of those who handed him over, who denied him, who were afraid to come close to his power. His compassion was present not only in all the times when he fed, healed and raised folks from the dead. His compassion was also manifest in that moment when he took pity on the weakness of those who would do him wrong.

**Thea:** What manner of man is this....

**Bede:** And so we have the great paradox, the great stumbling block of Black Theology and of African American culture. We see the still point upon which rests so much pain, resentment and confusion concerning some aspects of African American philosophy and ethics. How can you forgive your enemies? How could Martin Luther

King, Jr., develop his theology of nonviolence? And expect others to follow it? How can the lamb lay down with the lion? Jesus did....

**Thea:** And so must we.

**Bede:** But there is another facet of the life and work of Jesus that is urgently needed right here in this discussion. Jesus was a prophet. Black Theology is a prophetic theology. African Americans are a prophetic people. "I heard from heaven today... I heard from heaven today."

**Thea:** And "everybody talking 'bout heaven ain't going there."

**Bede:** Girl, you got that right. That's slipping the prophetic word between the ribs of the soul, all right.

**Thea:** Bede, sometimes I get tired of having to remind people, even some of our own people, that black folks are not dumb. We have been twice as busy redefining the terms by which we live as other folks have been busy trying to trap us and trick us into thinking we had no way out of the valley of the shadow of death. How else can we make sense of something like: "Oh, I went into the valley/ and I didn't go to stay. But my soul got happy, Lord!/ And I stayed all day"? How you gonna stay all day unless God was shining down some mighty powerful heavenly light, allowing you to see the valley as nothing terrifying after all? It started out as the valley of the shadow of death and, before very long, it became a space as sacred as the mountain top.

**Bede:** The gift of prophecy in the black spiritual tradition demands that the same ruthless honesty be employed by the preachers and singers and prayers, as was employed by Jeremiah, Ezekiel, Hosea, Amos, Zephaniah and all the other old-time prophets. "Oh, Sinner, where you gonna run to?" "Oh, I went to the rock to hide my face." "Great God Almighty's gonna cut you down." "You call that a Christian? No, no, he scandalized my name."

**Thea:** That is exactly my point, Bede. Song after song puts the judgment squarely before us. You cannot help but know that you need to change your ways and admit how you have strayed from the pathways of righteousness when you hear somebody singing:

> *Sinner, please don't let this harvest pass;*
> *Sinner, please don't let this harvest pass;*
> *Sinner, please don't let this harvest pass,*
> *and die and lose your soul at last.*[6]

There is some mighty plain talk, as you well know, Bede, about the nature of sin and the proclivities of the sinner. Scandal-mongering, back-sliding—

**Bede:** And back-stabbing—

**Thea:** Lying, gambling, cheating, general disrespect and lowlife behavior—are all called to attention in the music. And sweet Jesus! the preaching at a black funeral, Bede! In *God's Trombones*, James Weldon Johnson captured only a taste of the laser-like quality black preachers employ when they delve into all sorts of sins, with the aim of rooting them out and making the sinner cry, "Mercy!"

**Bede:** And making many people sitting near the sinner squirm a little bit, too. But you were talking about the sermon in *God's Trombones* dealing with the prodigal son, weren't you, Thea?

**Thea:** Yes, I surely was.

> *Young man—*
> *Young man—*
> *Your arm's too short to box with God.*
>
> ....
>
> *Young man—*
> *Young man—*
> *Smooth and easy is the road*
> *That leads to hell and destruction.*
> *Down grade all the way,*
> *The further you travel, the faster you go.*
> *No need to trudge and sweat and toil,*
> *Just slip and slide and slip and slide*
> *Till you bang up against hell's iron gate.*[7]

And I think it is important to remember that, ultimately, these black believers tried to teach us that we have to look at even the worst sinner through the eyes of God. Why else fly up to the mercy seat and receive a consoling vision, if not to return to earth and tell the best news of all? "He's got the whole world in his hands."

**Bede:** "The faith that surpasseth all understanding" is a mighty hard gift to hold onto, Thea, for all of us. And maybe the greatest stumbling block the old ones carved up as a monument and testimony to their faith was the one called patience. To hang there on the cross, and not to call the angels to rain down fire from heaven—

**Thea:** "And He never said a mumbaling word"—

**Bede:** To look at all those people spread out beneath him, crowding and jeering around the cross—

**Thea:** "And He bowed His head and died"—

**Bede:** For Jesus to allow—to suffer—his death, well, Thea, that is a stumbling block, just like Paul said.

**Thea:** And for the Africans who took up the cross, to take up the patience of Jesus? That has been a stumbling block for many of their children, and their children's children, and for many another who has seen such patient endurance mark so many of us through the years.

**Bede:** If we are not patient, though, Thea, then they—the old ones—tell us that we just might miss the final word.

**Thea:** "He arose, He arose, he arose, just like he said."

**Bede:** Add patience to the list of Christian attributes, and finish off the list with resurrected. "In that great gittin'-up morning, fare you well, fare you well. In that great gittin'-up morning, fare you well." We are a resurrected people, after all. After all of the pain and suffering, and lying and betrayal, and abuse and violence—all the things that frighten and infect our world today, and affected their world back during the days of legal enslavement—they kept getting up, they kept resurrecting themselves. It was never a pious hope that someday, somehow, they would have a final meeting in the heavenly Jerusalem. No, they came back after the whip scars healed, after the amputations had stopped bleeding, after the initial heartbreak of seeing a loved one sold away had begun to subside. They came back when the running away failed. They came back when emancipation made them more unfree than ever. They kept getting up in the morning, moving from "can't to can."

**Thea:** We cannot have it both ways. We cannot worship a miracle-working savior and then deny him the power to work the greatest one of his ministry. We cannot weep in reverence, contemplating the heroic survival skills of the ancestors, and then call them foolish for believing in those very skills. When they declared, "Ain't no grave can hold my body down," they knew that they had already climbed out of the grave more than once, just to give the children some hope and to honor their elders who had chosen to survive.

**Bede:** That makes them a resurrected people, in my book. Am I right or am I wrong?

**Thea:** That is what the pages of my heart tell me, too. Let's sing the song, one more time, Bede. I feel filled up today, and I just have to sing about it.

> *God sent his Son, they called him Jesus;*
> *He came to love, heal, and forgive;*
> *He lived and died to buy my pardon,*
> *An empty grave is there to prove my Savior lives.*
>
> *Because He lives I can face tomorrow;*
> *Because He lives all fear is gone;*
> *Because I know He holds the future,*
> *And life is worth the living just because He lives.*
>
> *How sweet to hold a newborn baby,*
> *And feel the pride, and joy He gives;*
> *But greater still the calm assurance,*
> *This child can face uncertain days because He lives.*
>
> *Because He lives I can face tomorrow;*
> *Because He lives all fear is gone;*
> *Because I know He holds the future,*
> *And life is worth the living, just because He lives.*

And then one day I'll cross the river;
I'll fight life's final war with pain;
And then as death gives way to vict'ry,
I'll see the lights of glory and I'll know He lives.

Because He lives I can face tomorrow;
Because He lives all fear is gone;
Because I know He holds the future,
And life is worth the living just because He lives.[8]

## For Reflection

- Think of your relationship with God, beginning when you were very young. In what ways have you changed the way you rely on God? How you speak with God?

- Consider changes that are presently occurring in your life. Imagine yourself standing at the crossroads. To whom do you speak, asking for guidance and insight? What would you say?

- Are there people in your life, in your community, who could benefit from your standing with them at their crossroads? In what ways could you help?

- Reflect on the qualities of righteous Christian life discussed in this meditation. Spend some time thanking God for the ways each of these virtues has been manifested in your life. Also, thank God for those who have symbolized these virtues for you. Make a commitment to embody patience in a particular way that will draw you closer to Jesus.

## Closing Prayer

Dear sister Thea and brother Bede, we rejoice in the steadfastness with which you strove to serve God, giving all you had until you had no more to give. Nourished by your wisdom and by the songs you lived as your life, we thank God for your gifts to us. We ask God to so enrich us that we might be gifts to the world as well. Amen.

## Notes

1 William Gaither, "Because He Lives," *Baptist Hymnal* (Nashville: Convention Press, 1991), #407.

2 In *Moses, Man of the Mountain*, Zora Neale Hurston presents the best example of African American creativity appropriating the stuff of culture and transforming the material into work that provides a fresh insight into the original material, and into the newly faceted result. Hurston's rendering the myth of Moses in "Negro Speech" is a success of fiction, folklore and spirituality. See "Moses, Man of the Mountain" in *Hurston: Novels and Stories* (New York: The Library of America, 1995), pp. 337 ff.

3 "What Manner of Man Is This." *Mahalia Jackson: Volume 2.* Columbia/Legacy. C2K 48924. Disk One.

4 Roger D. Abrahams has selected many African and African American folktales which would illustrate this point, and which could be useful in many other contexts as well. See *African Folktales* (New York: Pantheon Books, 1983) and *Afro-American Folktales* (New York: Pantheon Books, 1985).

5 Romans 25, in Toni Morrison, *Beloved* (New York: Plume Books, 1987). In this work, Morrison demonstrates how selfishness at a time of great crisis can cause a group of individuals to forget the teaching of the elders (in the person of Baby Suggs) and destroy the lives of children (the infant daughter of Sethe). Morrison is also profoundly therapeutic in showing how a community is formed when these same individuals admit they have broken the covenant with their past experiences, and join in a circle of atonement.

6 *Lead Me, Guide Me*, #172.

7 James Weldon Johnson, *God's Trombones: Seven Negro Sermons in Verse* (New York: Penguin Books, 1976), p. 21.

8 "Because He Lives," op. cit.

# Day Six
## Working on a Building

### Coming Together in the Spirit

In the great spiritual text, the *Narrative of Sojourner Truth*, an illuminating story is recorded of an instance where, after some fervent praying, Sojourner Truth, armed only with conviction and a song, quelled a mob of dangerously unruly young men who were rampaging through a camp meeting near Northampton. More than a hundred young men, "with no motive but that of entertaining themselves by annoying and injuring the feelings of others," ran wild through the grounds, while those assembled for prayer and revival cowered in the tent, or hid from the running mob. Sojourner Truth hid herself behind a trunk in "the most retired corner of a tent." After much soul-searching prayer, she decided to confront the mob. Even though she felt herself in danger, being the only black person on the grounds, she reasoned with herself thus:

> Shall I run away and hide from the Devil? Me, a servant of the living god? Have I not faith enough to go out and quell that mob, when I know it is written—"One shall chase a thousand, and two put ten thousand to flight"? I know there are not a thousand here; and I know I am a servant of the living God. I'll go to the rescue, and the Lord shall

go with and protect me.

"Oh," said [Sojourner], "I felt as if I had *three hearts!* and that they were so large, my body could hardly hold them!"[1]

Sojourner emerged from hiding, vainly sought the aid of the camp meeting organizers and then proceeded to the heart of the storm by herself. What the *Narrative* next says about Sojourner Truth could just as easily be asserted about many of Thea Bowman's prophetic performances.

Sojourner left the tent alone and unaided, and walking some thirty rods to the top of a small rise of ground, commenced to sing, in her most fervid manner, with all the strength of her most powerful voice, the hymn on the resurrection of Christ—

> *"It was early in the morning—it was early in*
>   *the morning,*
>   *Just at the break of day—*
> *When he rose—when he rose—when he rose,*
>   *And went to heaven on a cloud."*

All who have ever heard her sing this hymn will probably remember it as long as they remember her. The hymn, the tune, the style, are each too closely associated with to be easily separated from herself, and when sung in one of her most animated moods, in the open air, with the utmost strength of her most powerful voice, must have been truly thrilling.

As soon as she started singing, Sojourner was ringed about by the entire mob of young men, most of whom were carrying clubs and sticks. She asked them why they were intent on doing her harm, since she intended none to them. They told her that they did not intend her harm. "We came to hear you sing," some said. Others said, "talk to us," and some others had stronger and stranger requests: "Pray, old woman. Tell us your experience." After she had them move back sufficiently—"You stand and smoke so near me, I cannot sing or talk," she said—she responded to each of their requests. The rapt attention of the crowd intensified to the point that, after several hours of singing, testifying and praying, Sojourner was able to disband the crowd. When she had made the entire assembly solemnly promise to disperse after one final musical request, she finished her night upon the stump with the following song:

> *I bless the Lord I've got my seal—to-day and*
> *to-day—*
> *To slay Goliath in the field—to-day and to-day;*
> *The good old way is a righteous way,*
> *I mean to take the kingdom in the good old*
> *way.*

Before the song was concluded many of the assembly had run away "like a swarm of bees" to the other tents, and to the other—scheduled—speakers, to be further instructed after their sudden conversion.

Prayer changes things.

## *Opening Prayer*

Almighty God, we kneel before you, knowing that it is still morning time in your creation, and we are still the merest children, dependent on your mercy, love and care. As we learn more about your ways and your desires for our fullness and happiness, we ask that we may learn to rejoice always in doing your will and in "taking the kingdom in the good old way." We pray with the Psalmist as we say, "Order my steps in Thy word, O Lord, and let not any iniquity have dominion over me" (Psalm 119:133). Amen.

# Retreat Session Six

**Thea:** We've talked about nothing else but prayer, it seems, Bede. So, maybe we ought to *talk* about prayer, now. What do you think?

**Bede:** I think we are going to talk about prayer. That's what I think, Thea. But what is specifically on your mind, that needs the searchlight of heaven's beam?

**Thea:** We pray that we might be changed. And then we pray that we might change things. That seems to be the starting point. "Walking and talking with Jesus" is not an eternally private and sheltered affair. No matter how long we "walk in the garden alone, while the dew is still on the roses," sooner or later we have to get back into the streets and face the world in the heat of the noonday sun. Sojourner Truth is a model for me; she always has been. She is a powerful witness for anyone who wishes to live a committed life, furnished by the Gospels. Until her mature years, Sojourner Truth lived the best she could, knowing very little of God and next to nothing of Jesus. She had a classic conversion experience, sensing God in the universe and within herself. The ecstatic moment overwhelmed her with a conviction of her own ingratitude in the face of the goodness of God. Sojourner thought that God would be justified in striking her out of existence because she had refused to rely on God for all things and to trust in his promises. Her experience of God, literally in "the wilderness," caused her to say: "Oh, God, I did not know you were so big," and to realize her life was forever changed.[2]

In story after story, we find the same thing.[3] Someone is

walking through the woods when suddenly a flash from heaven knocks them into another plane of existence, where a vision of heaven and hell opens before them. The immensity of the universe is measured from the perspective of God. The poor human child can see herself through the eyes of God, and must fall down in humble gratitude that she is allowed to exist.

**Bede:** "Oh, tell me how did it feel when you come out the wilderness, come out the wilderness, come out the wilderness? Tell me how did it feel when you come out the wilderness, leaning on the Lord?"

**Thea:** "Leaning on the Lord" is a beautiful and homely image of the covenant. "Leaning" implies a physical bonding, an intimate understanding of how our lives are connected to the power of God if we are to take any and every step. We could always stay in the wilderness, just as lost as a poor lost sheep. God gets us out of the wilderness—and, just like a friend, guides us gently to the right road. To the road of righteousness.

**Bede:** Prayer leads to a new way of seeing, a new way of living, a new way of acting. Am I right or am I wrong? Amen?

**Thea:** In the old days—and I suspect in these later days—most folks had to have a vision before they felt themselves ready to belong to the church. It is what we would understand as being "possessed by the Holy Ghost" today. Lots of times people would go off, if not to a real wilderness, at least to a graveyard, or some other secluded place where they could feel the presence of the beloved ancestors; and they would wait until they were caught up in their vision. After they had wrestled with their souls to absorb as much of the vision as they could contain, they would return to the community to tell the world "how [they] made it over."

**Bede:** That is the beginning of the prophetic life. Zora Hurston says: "The vision is a very definite part of Negro religion. It almost always accompanies conversion. It almost always accompanies the call to preach."[4] Once you come out the wilderness, you have to tell the world about it, you have to shout "the world over."

**Thea:** Exactly. Our every endeavor in—and encounter with—the presence of God is for the good of the community. When I reflect on the way Jesus prayed in the Bible, I am always struck at how the moments of quiet, "contemplative" prayer usually occurred right after he had worn himself out working miracles by the dozens—or right before he was about to experience another radical quantum leap into a new level of activity. He was constantly drinking from the fountain because being about his father's business made him develop a fierce spiritual thirst.

And then I think of how confused and conflicted the apostles were. They looked around and saw the disciples of John the Baptist just a-praying away—

**Bede:** They must have been like the sanctified folks, if they got that much attention—

**Thea:** And the apostles saw Jesus being fortified in those moments of his deep deep solitude—and so they finally took enough swallows of courage to approach him and ask him for some advice on how to pray. In Luke's account of the story, as soon as Jesus is finished telling the disciples how to structure their prayer, he launches into an example of the confidence that should spring from prayer.

> He was praying in a certain place, and after he had
> finished, one of his disciples said to him, "Lord,
> teach us to pray, as John taught his disciples." He
> said to them, "When you pray, say:
>
>> Father, hallowed be your name.
>> Your kingdom come.
>> Give us each day our daily bread;
>> And forgive us our sins, for we ourselves
>> forgive everyone indebted to us.
>> Do not bring us to the time of trial"
>> (Luke 11:1-4).

Jesus ends up the lesson by saying, "Ask, and it will be
given you; seek and you will find; knock and it will be
opened to you." Our praying ancestors stripped down
their prayer to the bare essentials, just like Jesus taught in
the Bible.

**Bede:** And their daily bread included "freedom."

**Thea:** You are most certainly right, my brother. In the
1960's the Freedom Riders took to changing one of the old
songs to say, "Woke up this morning and my mind, it was
stayed on *Freedom*," but I like to think that when the old
folks sang the version that said, "Woke up this morning
and my mind, it was stayed on Jesus," they meant the
same thing as the new one. Jesus *was* freedom, and they
had every confidence that when you asked for one, the
other one was delivered unto you.

**Bede:** One of the enslavement accounts has an old lady
say this:

> Marster neber 'low he slaves to go to chu'ch. Dey

hab big holes out in de fiel's dey git down in and pray. Dey done dat way 'cause de white folks didn' want 'em to pray. Dey uster pray for freedom. I dunno how dey larn to pray, 'cause dey warn't no preachers come roun to teach 'em. I reckon de Lawd jis' mek 'em know how to pray.[5]

**Thea:** They used to pray for freedom. And freedom came. But Jesus did more than free the shackles of slavery. God also freed the most open of the souls from greed, jealousy, anger, revenge, bitterness, despair—so many of the things that enslavement and the downright meanness of life would heap on the shoulders of many a believer. You can't ever truly be free until your soul and mind see things from the viewpoint of God. The chains can fall from the legs, and a person will stay where she is, because the chains have never been taken from her heart and soul and mind.

**Bede:** Amen. I know it to be true, Thea, I know it to be true.

**Thea:** Yes, Bede, my dear brother, I know you do. We both know the price we all pay when we keep the chains wrapped 'round our hearts. That's why we got to cry, "Holy, holy, holy, to the Lamb that was slain," before we can do a blessed thing for ourselves or for anybody else. Saying to God, "Hallowed by *your* name," first, shows gratitude. And there can be no freedom for anybody unless the person knows gratitude within his or her heart. Righteousness starts there: giving God the glory. Then we are truly in the right place at the right time—

**Bede:** Leaning on the Lord.

**Thea:** The reason for prayer is, ultimately, to remain close to God. We pray for grounding, and for grace; for bonding with God and with other believers, for renewal of our drooping spirits and our faltering hearts. But, first and ultimately, for spiritual union. Gratitude is the way we begin. When we express our gratitude to God for all the good things God has done for us, then we have a much better chance of understanding just what the Kingdom means when we pray for its arrival. No relationship is possible with anyone else unless gratitude is the atmosphere.

**Bede:** The scariest Christians I know are those who live every day as if they are already citizens of the Kingdom. Isn't this what we witnessed in our own lifetimes when we saw all those heroic people take to the buses, and to the streets, and to the lunch counters, and the drinking fountains, convinced that they were going to tear down the walls of Satan's kingdom? The Kingdom has to be in my heart and in my mind, pushing away the fear and the trembling that usually fill up our conscious days. The notion of Kingdom is prophetic also: the visions of the great prophets of the Bible tell us, over and over, of a picture of peace and union, of harmony. They tell us of a place where the widow and the orphan are cared for and called "beloved." They tell us of a city where the leaders preach peace. They tell us that oppression has been eradicated—

**Thea:**
> Where God "has scattered the proud in the
>     thoughts of their hearts,"
> where God "has brought down the powerful from
>     their thrones,
> and lifted up the lowly,"
> where God "has filled the hungry with good
>     things,

and sent the rich away empty." (Luke 1:51-54)

Oh, yes, the Kingdom looks nothing like the world of today. But we have to look on the world and see it as God intends it to be—without the blemish of sin. We who have carried the marks of sin upon our flesh, Bede, are signs of what the Kingdom must be in each individual. I told people, again and again: Don't look at me, with the marks of suffering and disease on my body, and see only the ravages of illness. Look upon me, see that I am wonderfully, fearfully made in the image of my God, and see what the possibility of all existence would be if we could remove the effects of sin from this world. I truly believe it, Bede, we must be about living in the Kingdom that Mary saw when she first got filled up with Jesus, and that Isaiah and Hosea and Ezekiel prophesied. We have to live the life we sing about in our song. Nothing can dissuade me from seeking the Kingdom in every shadowy corner of the world, and in every dark cave of the human heart. But it will availeth me not to pretend as if the shadowy caves do not exist.

**Bede:** That's another meaning of crossroads, I think.

**Thea:** Amen.

**Bede:** Each of us is an intersection of choices: good and evil, life and death, light and darkness, courage and fear, love and indifference, forgiveness and hatred, a spirit of sacrifice and a desire for vengeance—we carry the cross within us, the "thorn in the flesh," as Paul once said. I have to be aware every minute, every hour, that my redeemer lives and that my God can lead me out of the wilderness of my earthly desires and hungers. "Amazing Grace, how sweet the sound, that saved a wretch like me!"

Put my feet on solid ground.

**Thea:** Oh, yes, Bede. Yes. The daily bread we are taught to ask for has been leavened with the saving grace of God. It is a waybread for the soul, nourishment for the faltering heart. "Give us each day our daily bread." Jesus told those same followers, "I'm going to send you out on the road. Carry what you need, and just enough bread to live on each day." And that is what we need. I am not new in saying that the need for bread is also a cry for justice. In all those classes you taught on liberation theology, Bede, I know you preached this truth.

**Bede:** When we know that we are hungry, and that God's Kingdom will be a reorganizing of our human existence, that our basic needs are met and that we are gifted with abundance, then, indeed, our daily bread should be what we can reasonably expect and demand for others. The God of this Kingdom is a God who requires not a sacrifice but a loving and humble heart. This is the God who requires of us to "do justice, and to love kindness, to walk humbly with your God" (Micah 6:8). Well, I don't think much of that can be accomplished if we are lightheaded from a lack of bread. Nor will anything of grace be established if we are angry because we have been denied bread, or if we are distracted because we are so busy hoarding sustenance from the use of others, that we cannot afford to set a welcome table for all our sisters and brothers.

Our ancestors detailed all the great gifts of God, and in the one song that is a favorite of ours, Thea, they got as "down home," as possible. "I got shoes," they asserted. Even if the world conspired to deny or steal their gifts, they knew that God had given them what they were supposed to have in order to make the journey called life. They may have sung "heaven," but many of them knew that some quite specific "heaven" was just up the river, or a certain measurable number of miles northward. The prayer Jesus taught his disciples makes him sound as if his mama had herself been giving him some lessons in how to pray. It is not a far stretch from "sending the rich away empty, and filling the hungry with good things," to "give us each day our daily bread." Folks always say we learn our prayers at our mama's knee. That just might be especially true of Jesus. We may call that prayer the "Our Father," but there is a whole lot of "Our Mama" in that part about the bread. Am I right, or am I wrong?

**Thea:** You are as crazy as a prophet needs to be, Bede. And you are as right as the rain.

**Bede:** The version of the prayer that you used, the one appearing in Luke's account, has an interesting twist on the theme of forgiveness. We ask God to forgive us because we have already begun to forgive everyone who owes us something. Forgiveness is easily twisted up in our minds. It takes all the grace heaven can bestow to forgive those who have incurred our retribution. It means that the other has done something that would justify a punishment to be levied against him. It means that the other has unsettled the balance and must have some measure of her possessions taken away. It brings into the new Kingdom the notions of justice often found in the old kingdom. But Jesus wants us to say that we have already begun to write off the debt. We have our daily bread, why should we take any more than we need?

**Thea:** Because you know very well, my brother, that it is one of our most human hungers to see those who have wronged us feel our vindication. To be humble, after all, means to be lowly, insignificant, on the ground. It may be a virtue to sometimes lay down on the ground and lower ourselves in the presence of another, out of respect and wonder. It is another game altogether to demand of those who have wronged us that they must lie in the dirt and taste the ashes of our retribution, or, even worse, to be pushed into the dirt by someone who cannot stand up straight otherwise. Humility is not humiliation. And that is a game that we all are tempted to play, at some time. We can even call it justice, to ask that another taste the same dirt that we have been forced to swallow unjustly, year after year after year.

We can call it anything we want—and we often do. But we cannot call it acting like a child of God. And that is why, I think, Jesus taught us this prayer, this way. It is always about gratitude. God lifts us up from the dirt that is our starting place. How can we do less to those who have harmed us? I cannot help but think of the story of Sojourner Truth and the song she sang on the stump at the camp meeting:

> I bless the Lord I've got my seal—to-day and to-
> day—
> To slay Goliath in the field—to-day and to-day;
> The good old way is a righteous way,
> I mean to take the kingdom in the good old way.

"I mean to take the kingdom in the good old way." As long as I know that God is with me when I take the field, as long as I know that I can slay any demon or any giant adversary with what gifts God has already given me; as long as I know that I have already received my daily bread—well, then, I will let God take care of the rest. Martin Luther King, Jr., taught it well, when he advised his followers in the ways of nonviolence. Never descend into the gutter except to help someone out of it. Never stoop to lower yourself. Establish the standard by which others should behave. That is what the prayer means when it says, "as we ourselves forgive." God has established the standard by which we are to act. God has forgiven us. And that's that. Any other behavior would demonstrate the rankest ingratitude.

**Bede:** The prayer is a prayer of the crossroads, too. "Lead us not into temptation." You know, the old folks sure could talk about the devil, could get all in his business. They would have fun in church, singing and acting out the ways of the devil and his foolishness. "The devil is a liar and a conjurer too; if you don't watch out, he'll conjure you." "Better mind my sister (brother), how you walk on the cross; your foot might slip and your soul will be lost." We can get all turned around at the crossroads of our lives. So, leaving nothing to chance or rattled brains, we ask God to make sure he intervenes and does not allow us to slip off the cross—take the wrong path.

**Thea:** Because we have somewhere to go, some work to do, some goals to achieve. We've got to take the Kingdom the good old way. Now, Bede, I am thinking of another great old gospel song that you and I both have sung many a time, a song that puts our "kingdom taking" in a wonderful light. Sing it, with me.

> *I'm working on the building*
> > *(working on the building)*
> *True foundation*
> > *(true foundation),*
> *Holding up the blood-stained*
> > *(holding up the blood-stained),*
> *banner for my Lord*
> > *(banner for my Lord),*
> *Soon as I get through*

*Working on the building*
　　　　*(working on the building),*
*Going up to heaven*
　　　　*(going up to heaven)*
*Get my reward.*


*You hear me singing*
　　　　*(working on a building),*
*Working on a building*
　　　　*(working on a building),*
*Holding up the blood-stained*
　　　　*(working on the building),*
*banner for my Lord*
　　　　*(working on the building).*
*Just as soon as I get through*
　　　　*(soon as I get through),*
*Working on the building*
　　　　*(working on the building),*
*Going up to heaven*
　　　　*(going up to heaven),*
*Get my reward.*

*That's why I'm working on the building*
　　　　*(working on the building),*
*Holding up the blood-stained*
　　　　*(holding up the blood-stained)*
*banner for my Lord*
　　　　*(banner for my Lord).*
*Just as soon as I get through*
　　　　*(soon as I get through),*
*Going up to heaven*
　　　　*(going up to heaven),*
*Get my reward.*[6]

**Bede:** God is a good God! Amen.

**Thea:** Amen. Hallelujah! Bede. The prayer we do is the way we get our daily bread, and the bread provides the strength we need to work on the building, which is the Church, which is the family, which is the world, which is the Kingdom. Which is ourselves. Unless God provides the grace, the labor we do is in vain. And unless we pray, and work, and sing, and dance, and lift each other up in gratitude, all our endeavors are in vain.

**Bede:** Amen. And thank you, my sister.

**Thea:** Bless God.

## *For Reflection*

- *We are a resurrected people. Look back over your life and recount some of the many resurrections from the tomb you have experienced.*

- *Look at where you feel most trapped and burdened today. Ask Jesus to come to this place and "roll the stone away," bringing a new sense of freedom to your life.*

- *We each need our daily bread, and we are called to provide nourishment—both material and spiritual—for others. In what circumstances have you been given unexpected nourishment through the lives of others? For whom have you provided such nourishment for others? Spend a few moments thanking God for giving you the gifts you share with others.*

- *Where in your life have you experienced the all-encompassing forgiveness of God? The forgiveness of* others? Where do you most need to pray for the grace to forgive another today?

- Sit and talk with Jesus, asking for the grace to "see the world through the eyes of God." As you experience the brokenness of the world, what gifts would you ask from God, so that you might be helping to make the Kingdom come?

## Closing Prayer

Good and gentle God, you are Mother and Father to us. Lead me, guide me along the way, for if you lead me I cannot stray. In the moments of darkness, wilderness, and doubt, let me feel your care and your steadfast presence. My entire life and all I possess are gifts from you, O God, and my gratitude for your continual love overwhelms my soul. Teach me to remember your ways, and may your praises be ever in my heart and on my lips. Amen.

### Notes

[1] The story is taken from *Narrative of Sojourner Truth* (New York: Oxford University Press, 1990) as part of The Schomburg Library of Nineteenth-Century Black Women Writers, Henry Louis Gates, Jr., gen. ed., pp. 115-117.

[2] *Narrative of Sojourner Truth*, p. 66.

[3] A useful introduction to the world of conversion narratives is *God Struck Me Dead: Religious Conversion Experiences and Autobiographies of Ex-slaves*, ed. Clifton H. Johnson (Philadelphia: Pilgrim Press, 1969).

[4] Zora Neale Hurston, *The Sanctified Church* (Berkeley, Calif.: Turtle Island Press, 1983), p. 85. This collection of Hurston's writings on religious practices and beliefs is a valuable resource. Much of the same material can also be found in *Zora Neale Hurston: Folklore, Memoirs, and Other Writings* (New York: Vintage Books/The Library of America, 1990).

[5] Ellen Butler, in *Bullwhip Days: The Slaves Remember: An Oral History*, ed. James Mellon (New York: Weidenfield & Nicolson, 1988), p. 190.

[6] This song has been adapted from the performance of Brother Joe May (with the Sallie Martin Singers), found on *Brother Joe May: Search Me Lord*, Blues Interactions, Inc., 1991, PCD-1824. Another compelling performance can be found on *Marion Williams: Strong Again*, Spirit Feel Records, 1991, Spirit Feel 1013.

# DAY SEVEN
## Finding a Balm in Gilead

### Coming Together in the Spirit

From June 1989 until her death in March 1990, Sister Thea Bowman gave a testimony to the power of believing that the Kingdom is already here, and she provided this testimony in gatherings both large and small, and from her sickbed. Her address to the National Council of Catholic Bishops (NCCB), on June 17, 1989, remains a beacon of Black Catholic (Southern, Womanist) Theology. To answer the question, "What does it mean to be black and Catholic?" Thea, sitting in her wheelchair, kept warm by a quilt draping her shoulders, began singing, "Sometimes I feel like a motherless child."[1]

Those who would have been intimidated by her illness, for whom the sight of anyone in a wheelchair would have been sufficient cause to fling open the floodgates of pathos and sentimentality, were quickly whipped into rational alertness. Thea did not present herself to the bishops to gain their pity or compassion. She rolled up on the shores of their assembly to show them a woman who continued to exist because of a fully formed spirituality and whose sustenance and "medicine" was to do the will of God.

The woman in a wheelchair once again relied on a line from an old spiritual to describe what she was about that day. "I keep so busy serving my master," Thea said, "I ain't got time to die." She called the bishops to an authentic integration of the Church in which the gifts of all would be respected and fully invested. She called them to walk together with all their brothers and sisters toward that new Church which was yet a long way off. And, at her request, the bishops responded by standing, crossing their arms, holding each others' hands, and singing "We Shall Overcome."

Comments she made during an interview for *Praying* magazine, at the end of 1989, illuminate this facet of her spirituality:

> ...Part of my approach to my illness has been to say I want to choose life, I want to keep going, I want to live fully until I die....
>
> I don't know what my future holds. In the meantime, I am making a conscious effort to learn to live with discomfort, and, at the same time, to go about my work. I find that when I am involved with the business of life, when I'm working with people, particularly with children, I feel better. A kind of strength and energy comes with that.[2]

An event between her address to the NCCB and her interview with *Praying* can serve to bring this act of faith into a remarkable and dramatic focus. On the morning of July 4, 1989, the entire community of the Institute for Black Catholic Studies boarded three buses and left New Orleans, Louisiana, for Canton, Mississippi. It was the second summer during which Sister Thea had been unable to teach her full load of courses, so the leadership of the Institute decided to have its annual "Founders' Day" celebration in Thea's home. More than 150 people of every age, ethnic background and status imaginable filled up the pews of Holy Child Jesus Church and began the celebration with prayer, song, story-telling and general foolishness. Sister Dorothy Kundiger brought Thea into the assembly, and the circle formed around the two women. With Thea's arrival, the assembly became sisters and brothers to one another on a level much more profound than could be achieved during a regular summer school session.

The celebration was a good example of conservative black culture at its best. The feeling of ritual was everywhere present. Old songs were sung. Participants told old stories, old jokes. Anecdotes of a shared past were brought up, once again. The newest students and faculty were hurled into an immersion tank of communal healing. It was obvious to many, if not all, that this celebration was simultaneously a "homecoming," a testimonial and a "leave-taking." It was the most sacred of all black rituals: a family reunion.

And, since the ritual existed with Thea Bowman at the center of its circle, eventually it was a time for the "true truth" to be told. She took the microphone, and she proceeded to bless the assembly and to "bless out" the assembly, once again adjusting the mantle of prophetic black womanhood upon her shoulders. The "old lady" had a few words to say to her "chil'ren," and, by the grace of God, the children—all assembled—were going to hear every blessed word.

Thea commented on each contribution (and on many of the contributors). She told her own stories about moments of foolishness, and shared pains and common triumphs. There were praise and admonishments. There were moments of utter, profound, holy quiet. What she did not say, she showed. Thea had come to the celebration soon after having endured another round of radiation treatments. The drawn guide-marks for the tubes were still visible on her skin. The thinness of her body, the frailty of her gestures were also part of her preaching that day. As she said in that later interview: "In the meantime, I am making a conscious effort to learn to live with discomfort, and, at the same time, to go about my work."

But what she said that day was her own paraphrase of the three letters of John: "Little children, love one another." Ah, then, we must consider what she sang.

All through her public career, one of Thea Bowman's favorite songs was "Done Made My Vow to the Lord." As is true of most of the sacred—and not so obviously sacred—songs of the African American tradition, much of the meaning of this song depends on the context it which it is sung and heard. Some songs take on radically different meanings if they are performed at a fast tempo, as opposed to a slow beat. Some songs (and this one is a good example) can change their meaning depending on the age of the singer, or a host of other particularities. To hear Thea Bowman sing this song in the days of her prime health was a different experience than hearing her sing it when her breath support was weakened by the aftermath of cancer surgery and treatment.

And to hear Thea Bowman begin this song, on July 4, 1989, months before her death, was to hear a new meaning erupt in the soul like a revelation at Pentecost. She asked all the small children in the church to come and stand by her. She reached out and held the hands of those nearest her, and she sang:

*Done made my vow to the Lord,*
*And I never will turn back,*
*Oh I will go, I shall go*
*to see what the end will be.*

*Sometimes I'm up, sometimes I'm down; See what*
*the end will be,*

*But still my soul is heav'nly bound, See what the
end will be.*

*Done made my vow to the Lord,
And I never will turn back,
Oh I will go, I shall go,
to see what the end will be.*

*When I was a mourner just like you; See what the
end will be,
I prayed and prayed 'til I came through, See what
the end will be.*

*Done made my vow to the Lord,
And I never will turn back,
Oh I will go, I shall go,
to see what the end will be.*[3]

Thea Bowman absorbed the energy of those who had journeyed to Canton to get energy from her, and she transformed it into a healing ritual: a healing touch, a cleansing word, a blessing with a sacred song. Thea made the mourners mourn, and then forced them to look at her with the eyes of her own faith. The true truth was this: Stepping off into glory, she still had the faith to work miracles for others. She was a teacher, a prophet and a woman who never, never, never turned back.

## *Opening Prayer*

O, God, who art great and good, incline your ear toward me this day, and pour upon me the grace of your healing power. Strengthen my weak and faltering spirit; bring relief to the pains of my heart and soul and body. As we remember the life and struggles of Sister Thea, help us to learn the lesson she strove to teach us: that we must live until we die, and that our dying is truly a crossing over into your tender love. As we stand in the presence of our brother, Bede, help us to learn what you taught him in his life: that we can never give up our hunger and thirst for your forgiveness, mercy and love. In the name of Jesus, we pray. Amen.

## RETREAT SESSION SEVEN

**Bede:** All the talking we have done about the sacred music of our people has put into my mind an African theory of healing, Thea. What I am talking about is the Kongo tradition of making objects that possess the ability to heal those who rely on them. Those objects are called *minkisi*.[4]

**Thea:** Now, Bede, you are not about to run off into some voodoo woods, are you?

**Bede:** You and I both know that the stereotypes that stick to African healing sciences and to African spirituality are enough to bring shame to people who otherwise seem educated.

**Thea:** That's the truth, Bede. And I know just what you are talking about. Our ancestors believed that the right drum rhythms could heal a person, and that the wrong rhythms could disturb whole communities of people. They believed that if you very carefully studied what imbalances there might be in somebody's life, you could collect the right ingredients to restore that balance and cure the person. Now, anybody who wants to call that witchcraft or voodoo is welcome to say the same thing about every pill in the medicine cabinet and every visit to a mental health care professional. Too many of our illnesses and diseases are due to some sort of physical or mental imbalance. It would be wrong to condemn in others what we value in ourselves.

**Bede:** These traditional sacred objects have some ironic similarities with some of the devotional items we Catholics have always relied on. I mean, things like medals, holy cards, rosaries, scapulars, relics: all those items we know have some special power associated with them and which we use for the restoration of health and peace of mind.

**Thea:** Objects with an historical and spiritual value in the community, and to which are often attributed the power to heal. Is that what you are saying, Bede?

**Bede:** That's it. These African objects are really receptacles of objects, and the container is usually a bag or some sort of tied-up cloth. Inside could be bits of dirt, or feathers, or shells, or artifacts or mementos associated with some person of great power and who is held in great affection by the people or the community. The person who put all of this together would be the spirit-specialist, a well-trained individual whose gift was, in reality, the discernment of spirits. Now—and this is where I begin to believe that our spirituality is reinforced by our being Black and Catholic—we know that in the Roman Catholic Church we have long held that the intercession of saints and the devotions surrounding the relics of these holy women and men should be practices greatly respected and taught to our children. Our community of believers have always known that holiness resides in human vessels and in material objects.

**Thea:** And by "our community" you mean our black community and also our Catholic community.

**Bede:** I do.

**Thea:** So, if I can swing my intuition into play, you are implying that, somehow, our sacred music should be reverenced like relics or devotional objects, or like these *minkisi* you have described.

**Bede:** I mean just that. And I have gained that meaning from watching you sing, over the years, and from studying the history of—and the devotional respect given to—our sacred songs. Think about it. When our community has been in deep trouble, when there is something unbalanced in the church, for instance, somebody will get up and sing one of the old songs—and offer that song so that some balance, some harmony, can be restored to the people who are in turmoil or trouble. Look at the use of the Spirituals in the Freedom Rides and marches of the the 1950's and 1960's. When folks, old and young, hale and frail, walked into the midst of the hate-soaked mobs, you know they were deeply afraid, "troubled in mind," to the extreme. Then somebody sounded off, "We shall overcome...we shall overcome...."

They didn't mean that in some sort of eschatological dream state. They meant, "we shall overcome our fears, doubts and anxieties in this spot, in this moment; here and now, we shall overcome the threat of immediate and ugly death." And they did overcome. What they were able to overcome, they did as a legacy for all of us—their descendants and for the descendants of the mob, too. That song, whenever it is sung, wherever it is called into a community's consciousness, has the power to bring up the memory of those freedom warriors, and to instill in us some of their power to overcome the forces of darkness (within and without).

**Thea:** Amen, Bede. Amen. I'm a witness to the power of the song. Some days, when it hurt me to breathe, I could find a way to hum a song, or even sing one—and I could hold some of the pain at bay. Sometimes I could almost forget about the pain when I was performing the old songs.

**Bede:** I am convinced those songs were composed with that intention by those who first sang them.

**Thea:** Years ago, James Cone shared the soul of these songs with us when he said:

> [The spiritual] invites the believer to move close to the very sources of black being, and to experience the black community's power to endure and the will to survive.... I affirmed the reality of the spirituals and blues as authentic expressions of my humanity, responding to them in the rhythms of dance. I, therefore, write about the spirituals and the blues, because *I am the blues* and *my life is a spiritual.* Without them, I cannot be.[5]

In many ways, this interpretation of the music as being an object that heals is very old, almost commonsensical wisdom. I think you are right, Bede. The old folks were denied or forbidden the right to read, to write, to communicate freely. In many places, you could be killed if you even attempted to teach another these basic skills. And some of the greatest so-called Christians in the community were the first to whip, maim or kill anyone who tried to worship the Christian God. The information necessary for survival and for cultural development had to be transmitted somehow. I am thinking of the heartbreaking lullabies sung to black children who were placed in a basket under a tree, while the mama was in the kitchen taking care of somebody else's child. How to soothe your crying child when you can't even reach out your hand and touch your baby? Any song that could cut through that pain and alienation has to have some healing power.

**Bede:** Take the situation and turn it around. That is how we have been healed and how we are called yet to heal.

**Thea:** There is a song—

**Bede:** Amen. There always is, praise God!

**Thea:** —that could pull all of this together.

*There is a balm in Gilead, to make the wounded whole,*
*There is a balm in Gilead, to heal the sin-sick soul.*

*Sometimes I feel discouraged, And think my work's in vain,*
*But then the Holy Spirit Revives my soul again.*

*There is a balm in Gilead, to make the wounded whole,*
*There is a balm in Gilead, to heal the sin-sick soul.*

*Don't ever feel discouraged, For Jesus is your friend;*
*And if you look for knowledge, He'll ne'er refuse to lend.*

*There is a balm in Gilead, to make the wounded whole,*
*There is a balm in Gilead, to heal the sin-sick soul.*

*If you cannot preach like Peter, If you cannot pray like Paul,*
*You can tell the love of Jesus, And say "He died for all."*

*There is a balm in Gilead, to make the wounded whole,*
*There is a balm in Gilead, to heal the sin-sick soul.*[6]

I feel that this song illustrates a good definition of a sacramental: It is a sacred sign through which spiritual effects are obtained by the intercession of the community of believers. When you hear this song, when you sing this song, you feel the healing that the song talks about. There is something more: This song teaches us how to get busy *acting* healed. It has a prophetic element built into it.

**Bede:** Reading the song brings a renewed appreciation for the theological abilities of our ancestral singer/composer mystics. The reference to a "balm in Gilead" is not what most might think. In the Book of Jeremiah the references have a different import. Gilead is mentioned three times in Jeremiah.

> Is there no balm in Gilead?
> Is there no physician there?
> Why then has the health of my poor people
> not been restored? (Jeremiah 8:22)

> For thus says the Lord concerning the house of the
>     king of Judah:
> You are like Gilead to me, like the summit of
>     Lebanon;
> but I swear that I will make you a desert, an
>     uninhabited city. (Jeremiah 22:6-7)

> Go up to Gilead, and take balm,
> O virgin daughter Egypt!
> In vain you have used many medicines;
> there is no healing for you. (Jeremiah 46:11)

You don't even have to be a scholar of Scripture, Thea, to see that these references consider the region of Gilead to be a center of medical learning and practice. It would be like us saying, "Are there no specialists at the Mayo Clinic!" Gilead is a place special in the concern of God, the prophet says. Accordingly, the prophetic metaphor likens

Israel's alienation from God to be like a patient going to
Gilead, carrying her own medicine. Jeremiah is implying
that all the balm in Gilead cannot heal the sick person, and
not all the compassion of God can change the heart of
Israel. If the sin and illness manifested by Israel are of
such terrible consequence that not even all the medicines
of Gilead can heal them, then they will be punished on
such a level of magnitude that it would be as if the lush
and bountiful lands of Gilead and Lebanon had been
made into deserts.

**Thea:** And then, Great God! the singer/composer declares
that there was enough balm in Gilead, after all. That there
was enough faith and humility and integrity for the
therapy to work. Jeremiah asked a rhetorical question, and
the Spiritual-artist turned the question around. Answering
Jeremiah—and by implication, God—the singer asserts
that the desert of doubt and the wasteland of despair have
been made green and productive. I think of this song as a
companion to "This Little Light of Mine." The ability to
claim personal power in the Kingdom of God is a radical
act of freedom. It may not be much, but this little light of
mine will dispel the darkness around (or within) me; that
much I know. Further, since "God gave it to me," I will let
it shine "everywhere I go."

"Balm in Gilead" does the same thing. It even speaks
a word of comfort to the prophet Jeremiah. Don't worry,
child of God, the song says. We came through the desert,
so there don't have to be any more deserts. We came
through the darkness, so there never needs to be any more
fear of the dark. We have endured fire, water and blood,
so there never needs to be death-inducing pain in your
life. "Is there no balm in Gilead?" "Yes. There is a balm.
And it is sufficient for your needs." Whoever you are. I
want to throw my hand in the air when I hear a line like,

"If you cannot preach like Peter, if you cannot pray like Paul." The old folks wouldn't let nobody off the hook, would they, Bede? Don't come to me and say, "But we don't know how to sing like you, Sister Thea. We are not as learned and as eloquent as Father Bede. We don't clap our hands very well when we sing." God didn't let Moses or Jeremiah, or blessed Mary get away with that. And neither will any of us. "You can tell the love of Jesus, and say 'He died for all.'" Yes, indeed, there's no hiding place down here.

**Bede:** We have to say it over and over, Thea. The song makes us strong and it heals us by the sound and sense of it. "Let us break bread together"—

**Thea:** "On our knees, on our knees. When we fall on our knees and face the rising sun"—

**Bede:** Let us tell the love of Jesus. If God has got the whole world in his hands, then we have a lot of work to do, telling our healing song, giving witness wherever we find ourselves.

**Thea:** When the song says, "sometimes I feel discouraged, And think my work's in vain," I get filled up, Bede, knowing that every one of us can say that. The work of the Kingdom is never finished. And we wonder if we have ever accomplished all we could.

**Bede:** Oh, bless my soul. Amen.

**Thea:** That is why I kept singing my song, Bede. I made my vow to the Lord. And I really do think that at the many times of our discouragements, we have to remember that God is honored greatly by our fidelity. No matter in what "retired corner of the tent" we may find ourselves hiding from the devil's own mob, we have to find the same courage that convicted Sojourner to stand on a stump and tell stories, sing songs and pray the devil down. All we have is what God gave us directly and through the people, the beautiful, beautiful people. All God's children have something to give to each other. Find a word and preach it; find a song and sing it; find a love and share it.

**Bede:** There sure was a lot of stumbling and falling on our road to Bright Glory, wasn't there, Thea? I know I put a lot of scars on this battered old temple of the Holy Ghost. Rusty hinges and broken-down steps and all, we somehow kept on to see what the end would be. Hah! Praise God!

**Thea:** That's it, Bede. How can a soul fly away home if we never take our souls to heaven when we are living in the here and now? A song is the way to meet the angels and all who have gone on before, way in the middle of the air. Our spirituality makes the world into an infinite universe. We can go as far as the wings of faith can take us. And in faith we can never lose each other, or lose our way. Oh, Bede, I told many people my story about Sojourner Truth telling people how she wanted them to remember her death: "Tell 'em," she said, "that I went on home, like a shooting star."[7] But the stars of heaven were the focus of much of her spirituality, all through her life. She tells the story of how her mother taught her to keep her soul filled with hope in the midst of the deepest pain—that of being separated from all her loved ones.

Sojourner tells of her mother, burdened down with the anguish of a mother's love denied:

At times, a groan would escape her, and she would break out in the language of the Psalmist—"Oh Lord, how long?"... And in reply to [Sojourner's] question—"What ails you, mau-mau?" her only answer was, "Oh, a good deal ails me"—"Enough ails me."

Then again, she would point them to the stars, and say, in her peculiar language, "Those are the same stars, and that is the same moon, that look down upon your brothers and sisters, and which they see as they look up to them, though they are ever so far away from us, and each other."[8]

When Sojourner told her friends that she was going on home, "like a shooting star," she was talking about going home to be with her mother and father and sisters and brothers. She was going on, Bede, going on, to see what the end would be.

**Bede:** And the old ones told us about that, too, didn't they? After we have finished working on the building and go on to heaven to get our reward, they say, we will find out that there is "plenty good room in my Father's kingdom."

**Thea:** The reward of faithful service: "rest, in a place where there are rooms wid windows/ Openin' on cherry trees an' plum trees/ Bloomin' everlastin.'"[9] And where every bright and shining star that guided us through the nights of our lives will be discovered to have a face and a name—and we will know just how much loved and protected we were. It is very important for us to recognize the "cost of discipleship," Bede, just as it is of vital importance for us to remember that the reward of discipleship is even greater than the cost. There's plenty good room in the Kingdom.

**Bede:** Ultimately, the disciple's call is a call to "hold up the light, the beautiful light, down where the dewdrops of mercy shine bright." We are called to tell the truth when we lose our way, and to cry out for help when we stumble. We are called to make the right choice at the crossroads: life.

**Thea:** Always life. What else could we do, my brother? "I know I'll never turn back....the angels up in heaven done signed my name." And, you know, "We've come this far by faith, leaning on the Lord." So there's no way we're turning back.

**Bede:** What did you say, a minute ago? Find a word and preach it; find a song and sing it; find a love and share it.

**Thea:** And I would say this, too: The family needs to be healed. All of our family: Too many of our boy babies and girl babies and young women and men, too many mamas and daddies and sister-children and brother-children, and old ladies and old gentlemen, are lonely and hurting, and scared and tired. When your find your song—be a balm. When you finally claim your story, be a balm. When you let your light catch flame—be a balm.

**Bede:** Live the life you sing about in your song.

**Thea:** Thank God and bless you, too. I heard from heaven today. The angels up in heaven done signed my name.

**Bede:** Be a balm in Gilead.

**Thea:** Be a balm. Everywhere.

**Bede and Thea:** Somebody say "Amen."

## For Reflection

- *A gospel hymn asks the question, "is your all on the altar?" At this time visualize yourself walking to the altar in a private Offertory procession. What gifts would you place on the altar and dedicate to the service of God? What qualities of your life would you place on the altar, asking God to transform them and make them available to the world?*

- *Join in the conversation with Sister Thea and Father Bede. Spend some time thanking them for their presence during these meditations and asking them to intercede for you and your loved ones.*

- *Choose one of the songs that has meant a great deal to you and recite (or sing) it aloud. Hearing the word brings a spiritual power to us that is not achieved in just reading it. Do the same with any of the passages of dialogue that may have touched you in a special way.*

- *Speaking directly to the Holy Spirit, ask that you might see yourself as God sees you. Spend some time in thanksgiving and in petition that this retreat will bear fruit in your life.*

- *Call to mind those of your loved ones, your friends and acquaintances who might need the healing balm of Gilead in their lives today. Present them in prayer to God and ask that healing may be given them.*

## Closing Prayer

*There is a balm in Gilead, to make the wounded whole,*
*There is a balm in Gilead, to heal the sin-sick soul.*

*Sometimes I feel discouraged, And think my work's in vain,*
*But then the Holy Spirit revives my soul again.*

*There is a balm in Gilead, to make the wounded whole,*
*There is a balm in Gilead, to heal the sin-sick soul.*

## Notes

[1] The text of her speech can be found in *Sister Thea Bowman, Shooting Star: Selected Writings and Speeches*, ed. Celestine Cepress, F.S.P.A. (Winona, Minn.: Saint Mary's Press, 1993), pp. 29-37.

[2] Fabvienen Taylor, "Lord, Let Me Live Til I Die," *Praying* (November-December 1989), pp. 19-22.

[3] *Lead Me, Guide Me*, #285.

[4] A full explanation of the role of the *minkisi* in Kongo culture can be found in Robert Farris Thompson's *Flash of the Spirit: African and Afro-American Art and Philosophy* (New York: Vintage Books, 1983), and in Wyatt MacGaffey's *Art and Healing of the Bakongo* (Bloomington, Ind.: Indiana University Press, 1991). A good discussion on the west African beliefs of the healing power of music can be found in *The Healing Drum: African Wisdom Teachings* (Rochester, Vt.: Destiny Books, 1989), by Yaya Diallo and Mitchell Hall.

[5] James H. Cone, *The Spirituals and the Blues: An Interpretation* (Maryknoll, N.Y.: Orbis Books, 1991), pp. 5-7.

[6] *Songs of Zion*, #123.

[7] This story is recounted in John Ford's sermon, delivered at the funeral of Thea Bowman. It can be found in *Thea Bowman: Handing on Her Legacy*, ed. Christian Koontz (Kansas City: Sheed and Ward, 1991), pp. 24-29.

[8] *Narrative of Sojourner Truth*, pp. 17-18.

[9] "Sister Lou," in Sterling Brown's *The Collected Poems of Sterling A. Brown* (New York: Harper and Row, 1980), p. 54.

# Deepening Your Acquaintance

Nothing ever ends. No moment in our spiritual development is ever finished. The time spent with these two dear friends has brought us into the rhythm of the eternal. At times we have been lifted up, and at other times we have been brought quickly back to earth. The music that filled these pages and these prayers is the key to unlocking the secrets of black spirituality. We have learned to sing our souls into healing.

The themes presented in these meditations are not particular to Sister Thea Bowman or to Father Bede Abram. In fact, the process of composing these reflections took on the quality of a "heavenly dialogue." What is presented here is a collaboration in the truest sense. The voices of Thea and Bede were recognizable to my ear, and the issues they discuss in each of these meditations will be familiar to any reader who has heard any of us three speak.

It was a great education for me to share the classroom and the workshop podium with Thea and Bede. In a real way, we "made music together," like good jazz or church musicians. Each of us would play off the ideas and themes and images of the other. What Bede would say, Thea would use and then spin her own perspective, in her own way. When I would lecture, Bede would laugh and applaud and assent in his own unmistakable way. Later, he would use my ideas as references for his own wide-ranging commentary. We rejoiced in the work of each other.

This dynamic is present everywhere in the retreat. Many of the themes of my research and writing appear here. But the voices of Thea and Bede appeared within my head as I wrote down what seemed important to the three of us. The final reflection for these shared dialogues is partly disclaimer and partly exhortation.

Black spirituality is the inheritance of all who would drink from its fountain. Many great saints have given their hearts and souls and their creative gifts to the healing pool of this spirituality. I have given this book the essence of my research into the history of black spirituality. Thea and Bede gave their all at the altar of witness and teaching. From the three of us, this retreat has taken shape.

If you have gained any strength from these meditations, you must add to the treasure. Place your stories, your songs, your prayers and your desires into the dialogue as well. Tell the old, old story. Hold up the blood-stained banner for my Lord. Use this retreat as a model and help others develop songs to sing. Be a balm in Gilead.

And sing in exultation with and for your sisters and brothers:

*Tell me how did you feel when you come out the wilderness, Come out the wilderness, come out the wilderness?*

*How did you feel when you come out the wilderness, Leaning on the Lord?*

*I'm a-leaning on the Lord,*
*I'm a-leaning on the Lord,*
*I'm a-leaning on the Lord,*
*Who died on Calvary.*

*Loved every body when I come out the wilderness....*

*I'm a-leaning on the Lord....*

*Soul was so happy when I come out the wilderness....*

*I'm a-leaning on the Lord....*[1]

## Notes

[1] "Come Out the Wilderness," Princely Players (*Wade in the Water*).

# Resources

## Music

Because the entire retreat is based on an appreciation of black sacred song, the following collections of music are offered as an introduction and as aids to your prayer and reflections. Not all of the music used in this retreat is available on recordings. But any choir can learn any song. And members of the church can ask for music to be used during a church service, or request that new hymnals be purchased. More such involvement would aid our liturgies in unexpected ways. Besides the recordings listed here, you are encouraged to listen to the music of the great pioneers of the Negro Spirituals: Marian Anderson, Roland Hayes, Leontyne Price, Paul Robeson, the Tuskeegee Choir, the Fisk Jubilee Singers and others who kept the music alive during the first half of the twentieth century.

Kathleen Battle, Jessye Norman. *Spirituals in Concert.* Deutsche Grammophon. 429 790-2.

Thea Bowman. *Sister Thea: Songs of My People.* Krystal Records. KC009.

Thea Bowman. *Sister Thea: 'Round the Glory Manger: Christmas Spirituals.* Krystal Records. KC013.

*Precious Lord: The Great Gospel Songs of Thomas A. Dorsey.*

Various Artists. Columbia. CK 57164.

Charlie Haden and Hank Jones. *Steal Away.* Verve.
314 527 249-2.

Mahalia Jackson. *Gospels, Spirituals and Hymns.* Columbia.
C2K 47083.

_____. *Mahalia Jackson: Volume 2.* Columbia.
C2K 48924.

Sallie Martin Singers/ Cora Martin. *Throw Out the Lifeline.*
Specialty. SPCD-7043-2.

Brother Joe May. *Search Me Lord.* Blues Interactions Inc.
PCD-1824.

Odetta. *The Essential Odetta.* Vanguard Records.
VCD-43/44.

Opera Ebony. *Done Crossed Every River.* Arcadia.
ARC 2004-2.

Bernice Johnson Reagon, compiler. *Wade in the Water.*

*African American Spirituals: The Concert Tradition.*
Smithsonian Folkways. SF 40072.

*African American Congregational Singing.* Smithsonian
Folkways. SF 40073.

*African American Gospel: The Pioneering Composers.*
Smithsonian Folkways. SF 40074

*African American Community Gospel.* Smithsonian
Folkways. SF 40075.

Willie Mae Ford Smith, et al. *Mother Smith and Her
Children.* Spirit Feel. 1010.

Sweet Honey in the Rock. *Sacred Ground.* Earthbeat
Records. 9 42580-2

The Clara Ward Singers. *Meeting Tonight*. Vanguard.
145/46-2.

Marion Williams. *Strong Again*. Spirit Feel. 1013.

## Videos

### Thea Bowman

*Almost Home: Living with Suffering and Dying*. Ligouri
Publishing Co. 1989.

*Old-Time Religion*. Four videotapes. Treehaus
Communications. 1988.

### Bede Abram

*The Black Catholic Experience*. Four videotapes. The
Missouri Province Jesuits, 4511 West Pine Boulevard,
St. Louis, MO 63108-2191. 1988.

## Books

Bowman, Thea, ed. *Families: Black and Catholic, Catholic and
Black*. Washington, D.C.: United States Catholic
Conference, 1985.

Cepress, Celestine, F.S.P.A., ed. *Sister Thea Bowman,
Shooting Star: Selected Writings and Speeches*. Winona,
Minn.: Saint Mary's Press, 1993.

Koontz, Christian, ed. *Thea Bowman: Handing on Her
Legacy*. Kansas City: Sheed and Ward, 1991.

Listed here are a few basic resources that can help deepen

the appreciation for black spirituality and for the foundations of Black Theology.

Hayes, Diana. *And Still We Rise: An Introduction to Black Liberation Theology.* Mahwah, N.J.: Paulist Press, 1996.

Hopkins, Dwight N. *Shoes That Fit our Feet: Sources for a Constructive Black Theology.* Maryknoll, N.Y.: Orbis Books, 1993.

_____. and George Cummings. *Cut Loose Your Stammering Tongue: Black Theology in the Slave Narratives.* Maryknoll, N.Y.: Orbis Books, 1991.

Jones, Arthur C. *Wade in the Water: The Wisdom of the Spirituals.* Maryknoll, N.Y.: Orbis Books, 1993.

Spencer, Jon Michael. *Protest and Praise: Sacred Music of Black America.* Minneapolis: Fortress Press, 1990.

Thurman, Howard. *Deep River* and *The Negro Spiritual Speaks of Life and Death.* Richmond, Ind.: Friends United Press, 1975.

Walker, Wyatt Tee. *'Somebody's Calling My Name': Black Sacred Music and Social Change.* Valley Forge, Pa.: Judson Press, 1979.